TURNING BOXES AND SPINDLES:
STEP-BY-STEP

CONTENTS

INTRODUCTION

I have written this book to help the woodturner who already has some experience of turning, perhaps as a result of practising the techniques detailed in my first book, *Woodturning: Step-by-Step* (Batsford, 1993). In it I explore some of the possibilities of turning items with the grain running along the axis of the lathe. I start by describing in detail how to make a pestle and mortar, since this encapsulates the basic techniques of turning with the grain running this way, and go on to explore progressively more difficult projects each building upon skills that can be acquired by practising the preceding projects.

The methods I describe are not the only way you can turn these objects. There are as many different ways of turning as there are turners, and I have not tried to survey all the methods that can be used but have preferred to describe in detail those which I know work from personal experience.

I have acquired these techniques by working as a full-time turner since 1974 and, as a result of being largely self-taught, I have thought deeply about the whys and wherefores of everything I do. The advantages of this from your point of view is that you can rely on the fact that what I am describing is first-hand knowledge that is practical and that if you try my methods it will give you a firm practical foundation on which you can build your own personal variations.

PART ONE

BASIC TOOLS AND TECHNIQUES

Basic Tools and Techniques

In this book I do not describe in any detail how to equip the workshop as this is covered in *Woodturning: Step-by-Step*, but I do list the basic equipment you need; and in each project I add to this so that you can acquire the extra tools as and when you can.

EQUIPMENT

All the projects in this book can be done on a small lathe i.e. with a swing of 15 cm (6 in). Nevertheless, you do not need a small lathe to make small items and if you have the choice it is better to obtain as large a lathe as you can afford since you are bound to want to turn large objects eventually and large lathes tend to be more stable than small ones.

The other essential piece of equipment is a bench grinder for sharpening your tools. There is no greater bar to good turning than blunt tools and there is no better way of sharpening them than with an ordinary bench grinder fitted with one soft white aluminium oxide stone 60 grit size, medium to soft grade K for repairing or altering the profile of a carbon steel tool and one 100 grit aluminium oxide stone for creating a super sharp edge.

With regard to cutting up the wood prior to turning, the spindle turner is better served by normal timber suppliers than the bowl turner because timber is commonly sold in square-section stock and it is just a question of cutting it to length which can often be done with a handsaw. It is only when you seek to convert timber obtained in tree form (perhaps as a result of storm damage or from someone's garden rejects) or when you buy your timber in plank form that power saws such as chainsaws and bandsaws become necessary. These can be bought as the occasion demands and money supply allows and I give some guide lines in *Woodturning: Step-by-Step*.

BASIC TOOL KIT

At the beginning of each project I say what tools are needed. I refer to the basic tool kit and describe what additional tools are required. The basic kit is the set of spindle tools described in great detail in *Woodturning: Step-by-Step* and comprises a 31.25 mm ($1\frac{1}{4}$ in) roughing gouge, a 9.37 mm ($\frac{3}{8}$ in) beading and parting chisel, a 18.75 mm ($\frac{3}{4}$ in) oval skew chisel and a fluted parting tool (**fig. 1**). In addition to this you will need a rule, pencil, pair of dividers, external callipers, vegetable oil and beeswax.

ROUGHING GOUGE 31.25 MM ($1\frac{1}{4}$ IN)

This tool does the donkey work of converting square-section stock to a cylinder and its edge is square across the end. I describe how to use it in the pestle project. Like all the turning tools I use it has a concave bevel so that the edge can be supported by part of the bevel or the shoulder where the bevel meets the body of the tool and it can be used, as most turners do, direct from the grind stone. Extra sharpening with an oilstone can produce a very fine edge but can also tend to mar the concavity of the edge and is soon removed by the friction of the wood.

The roughing gouge is sharpened by holding the tool so that the sides

Fig. 1
Basic tool kit: (*from left to right*) skew chisel, fluted parting tool, beading and parting tool, roughing gouge, rule, pencil, vegetable oil, wax, dividers and external callipers

are parallel to the sides of the stone, and rotating it in the hand so that the whole of the bevel passes across the edge of the stone. You should always start grinding tools with the shoulder against the stone and work up to the edge so that only when you have nearly finished the grinding do the sparks come from the edge of the tool. You should never press the tool hard onto the stone because this causes the steel to overheat. You can tell that this has been done when the steel goes blue and this can only be corrected by grinding away the softened steel. If you need to do a lot of grinding of a particular tool you should frequently dip it in water to prevent it overheating.

When buying new tools you will

find that those made of high speed steel are more expensive than those made of carbon steel, but since they last much longer and need sharpening less often they do work out cheaper in the long run.

BEADING AND PARTING CHISEL 9.37 MM ($\frac{3}{8}$ IN)

This is a straight chisel made of 9.37 mm ($\frac{3}{8}$ in) square-section steel. It has two bevels square across the end and because it is narrower than the thickness of most grinding wheels does not have to be moved across the stone (i.e. from side to side). It therefore presents few sharpening challenges except that the angle of the bevels needs to be maintained. If either bevel gets too short the edge is not very fine and ceases to cut easily.

This tool is used in a motion that is common to some other tools, especially the skew (peeling cut) and is an up-and-over motion dictated by the need to have the bevel rubbing. You start with the tool pointing up, and as the cut progresses the tool goes further over the rest and then, as it nears the centre of the work, it points down below the level of the rest (**fig. 2**).

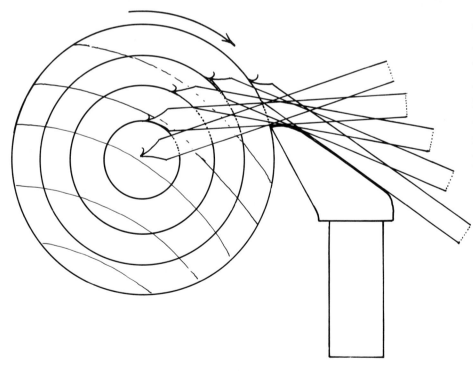

Fig. 2
Skew chisel, and beading and parting tool —
peeling cut

SKEW CHISEL 18.75 MM ($\frac{3}{4}$ IN)

The term skew chisel simply denotes a chisel with the edge ground at an angle to the long axis rather than square across. There are many different types of skew because of the variations possible in the angle and the stock from which the tool is made. In the photos you will see the type I prefer which is made from oval section high speed steel and has a curved profile. I use several of these because each has a different curve and is useful for particular purposes. I find that a skew with a long curved edge is useful for getting into narrow gaps, such as under rings, whereas a shorter edge is more useful for ordinary work.

The skew is sharpened in a similar way to the beading and parting tool except that since the edge is wider than the stone rim it must be passed along the rim and because the edge is curved the end of the handle must describe an arc so that the curve is maintained. The length of bevel plays an important role in the ease of cut and I am as prone as anyone to letting it get short, particularly when the wheel on my stone is getting worn down so that its diameter is too small. Every so often it pays to examine your tools with a critical eye and ask yourself whether the angle of edge and the length of bevel are really at their optimum. Be prepared to adjust these and try the altered tool out to make sure that it is working as well as it can.

The skew is a versatile tool that cuts in several different ways but it does so in such a way that if it is used properly it leaves a surface that needs little sanding. Its one drawback is that it is intolerant of bad handling and can be difficult to master. You may find that you can pick up the principles of its use from my books or failing that, a good teacher may help. However you learn it, it needs practice and more than any other tool you must handle it sensitively. You must not grip it too tightly. Then you can respond to what it is telling you about how it is cutting so that when the inevitable catch results you can let the tool be pushed from the wood rather than press it further into trouble.

The types of cut the skew is used for can be divided into three although once you have become familiar with the tool the distinctions between them become blurred and you move smoothly and seamlessly from one cut to another.

Peeling cut

This cut is used to remove a large quantity of material at speed in a narrow band (as the beading and parting tool does in an arc) from near the rest up and then down towards the centre. The tool has its wide face on the rest and the edge is parallel to the axis of the lathe. This cut generally leaves a ragged edge at the face of the cut at right angles to the axis.

Slicing cut

For this cut the narrow face of the tool is on the rest and either the

point or the heel (I always use the point) enters the work and cuts into the work across the fibres of the wood (**fig. 3**). This technique is used when cutting beads which start with a vee cut, the sides of which are widened one by one as the cut deepens. You can also use it to clean up the ends of spindles when it produces a very clean face which can only be improved by a variation of this cut known as the paring cut. Here the edge just behind the point is used with the bevel closely in contact with the face (**fig. 4**). The tool dips below the level of the rest down towards the centre of the work. The paring cut requires a great deal of concentration but produces a finish better than any abrasive.

The slicing cut is notorious for producing the skating catch where the tool shoots across the work in exactly the opposite direction intended, leaving a nasty spiral groove (**fig. 5**). I still do this when my attention wanders and this is when my pestles end up being thinner than usual. The reason for this species of catch is the usual one of not using the bevel to support the edge, probably because you are trying to remove too much wood at once and have accidentally allowed the tool handle to wander away from the correct angle to the axis. The difference between the correct angle and one that will cause a catch is very small with the skew, and this is why it takes so much practice to get it right.

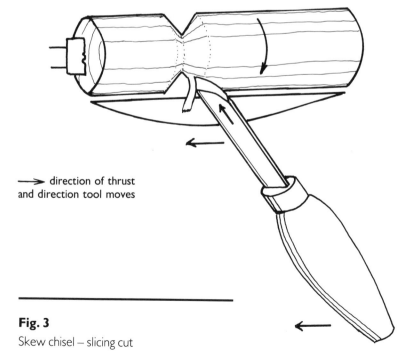

→ direction of thrust and direction tool moves

Fig. 3
Skew chisel – slicing cut

It is no good trying to stop a catch happening by gripping the tool tightly; if the tool decides to go there is no way that brute force will stop it. If you have a light grip you will find that you can feel whether the tool is cutting correctly and should be able to make the minute adjustments required to put things right. If you should lose control a light grip will enable you to take the tool away from the work before too much damage is done. It is a good idea to practise the catch and analyse what you are doing wrong. When you get to the point that you can do the catch at will you should be able to avoid it happening.

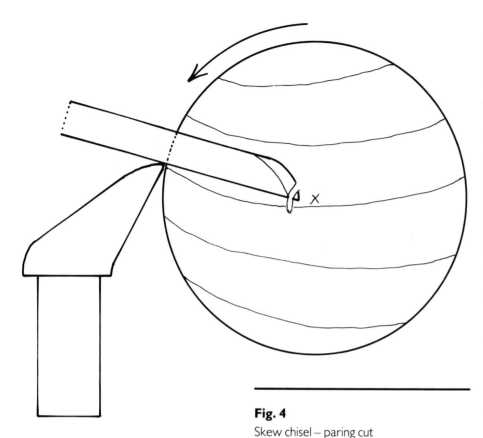

Fig. 4
Skew chisel – paring cut

Planing cut

When you want to produce a smooth, straight or gently-curved cylinder this is the ideal cut. This can be done either with the point up or down and as long as, first, the bevel is rubbing the work as the tool progresses along the work, and second, the edge is presented at about 45° to the axis, you will produce a good finish. The advantage of having the point down is that to achieve the correct angle the handle is way out to the side of the operator along the forearm and almost in a line with the direction of cut. When the point is up the tool needs to be almost at right angles to the axis in between the operator and the lathe so the sideways effort has to be done with a cocked wrist.

Once you have established the angle the tool needs to be held at, to take off a thin shaving and leave a good finish (whichever way you do the cut) you need to maintain this

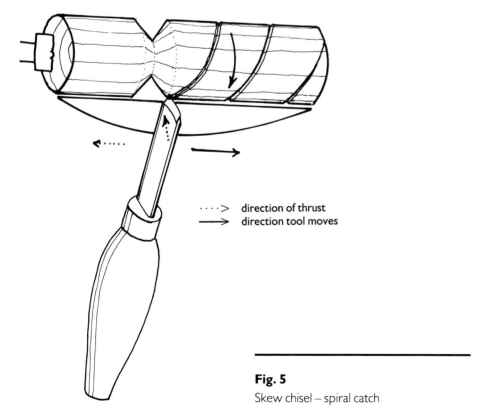

····> direction of thrust
——> direction tool moves

Fig. 5
Skew chisel – spiral catch

angle along the whole length without gripping the tool so hard that you cannot respond to the wood if you feel it needs a slight change of pressure or angle of cut.

The characteristic catch that occurs with this cut is the grab. When this happens the tool digs in, the edge is pulled down and the handle is forced up. The evidence on the work is a ragged hole and the cause is allowing the edge to lose the support of the bevel. In other words the handle has been held too high and the angle of the tool as a result is too steep (**fig. 6**). As with other catches the damage is worse if you are hanging onto the tool like grim death. If your grip is light the tool does not dig in so far and simply gets knocked away from the work. After all the wood is only saying that it will not be cut this way and is rejecting the tool.

FLUTED PARTING TOOL

This tool is used with the flute pointing downwards in an up-and-over cut as in the beading and parting tool and the skew peeling cut. It is designed for cutting deep grooves in the work and the spurs at each side of the flute cut the sides of the groove more smoothly than a conventional parting tool. It can be used for parting off, but I prefer the skew for this. I tend to use this tool for the limited number of occasions when I need a deep, straight-sided groove such as between bowls when I am making small bowls 'in the stack'. Its main drawback is that it tends to mark the rest and these grooves can impair the smooth progress of other tools along the rest. Because of the special uses of the tool I can live with having to file the rest occasionally.

BASIC KIT SUPPLEMENTS

I will explain the details of these tools as and when they are employed in individual projects because they have specialized uses. The exceptions are the half round and square ended scrapers and the spindle gouge used in several projects, and which I explain below.

Most of the other tools needed, such as those in **fig. 7** will be in the average tool kit. You will also need callipers and dividers. It is useful to have one pair of dividers, one pair of external callipers and one pair of internal callipers. The best types are with a spring on top and a screw to adjust the distance between the points. Dividers benefit from being sharpened when their points get blunt. The spanners are used for sizing and the mallet can be a bought carpenter's or a home-made carver's as in the photo.

Square ended scraper 12.5 mm ($\frac{1}{2}$ in)

This is a misnomer since the end is not exactly square but cut at a few degrees off the square and forms a dovetail when pressed straight into the work parallel with the axis. It is a standard tool but I sharpen it with a longer bevel than usual because I find that this cuts better. Not only do I grind the end off-square but also the left side so that it is not at right angles to the face of the tool. This ensures that the left hand corner is sharp and enables this point to go into narrow diameter holes such as along the inside of boxes right down to the bottom. If the side is square the bottom edge can foul the sides.

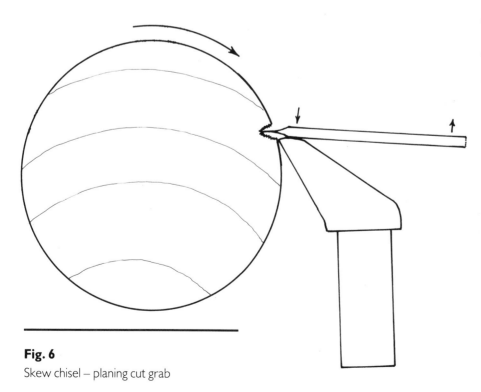

Fig. 6
Skew chisel – planing cut grab

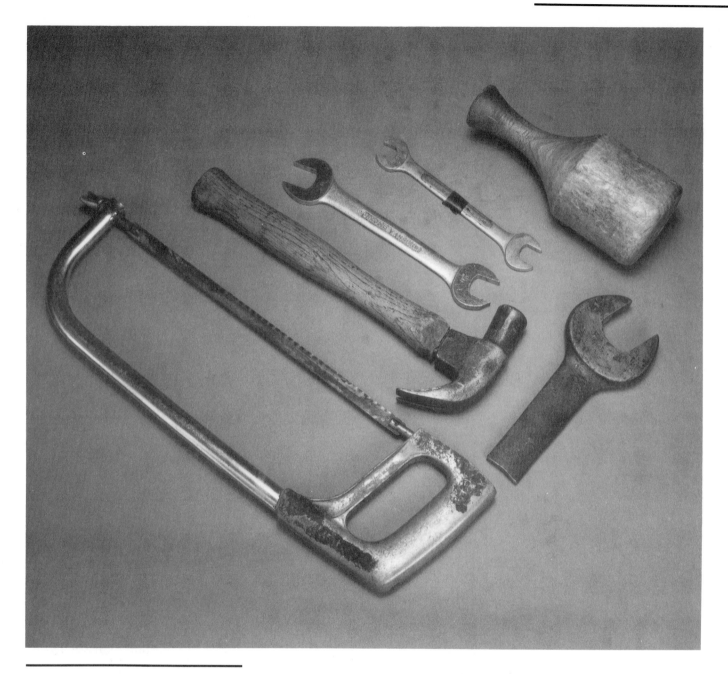

Fig. 7
Other tools: (*from bottom to top*) hacksaw,
hammer, spanners and carver's mallet

Half round scraper 37.5 mm (1½ in)

This is another standard tool but again I grind the bevel a lot longer than standard so that it can be used pointing upwards for the smoothing cut inside bowls. This gives a better finish off the tool than the normal way with the edge below the level of the rest, but it is a difficult cut for the novice and something only to be tried when you have sufficient confidence to handle the tool very lightly.

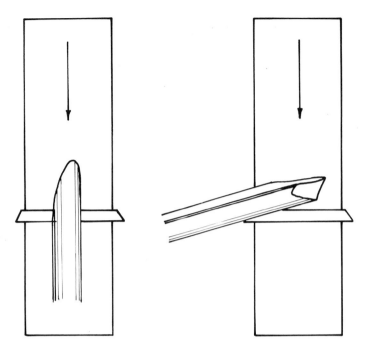

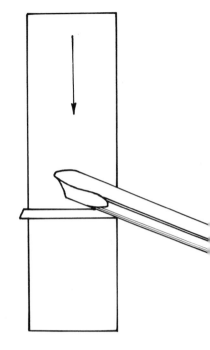

Fig. 8a
Sharpening nose of spindle gouge, tool
nearly horizontal

Fig. 8b
Sharpening long left hand bevel of spindle
gouge

Fig. 8c
Sharpening short right hand bevel of
spindle gouge

Spindle gouge 12.5 mm ($\frac{1}{2}$ in)

The spindle gouge has a shallow
flute and, for the way I use it, needs
to have a ground-back edge rather
like some bowl gouges. You can
then use it to hollow out end grain
and for this the only part that needs
to be ground back is the left hand
side if you turn between centres,
and the right side if you turn on the
outboard.

This is more difficult to sharpen
than the roughing gouge because
the tool needs to be passed through
140° so that the whole of the bevel
is ground with the rim tangential to
the edge (**figs. 8a–c**). This is so that
the marks left by the stone run from
the edge to the shoulder as though
they are radii of the curve of the
edge.

I describe how to use this tool in
more detail in the mortar project.

TOOL USE – GENERAL RULES

The only inviolable rule is to keep
your tools sharp. Blunt tools do not
cut cleanly and encourage you to
use more and more force to get the
tool to cut which can only end in
disaster. If you think your tool
might be blunt – sharpen it!

Most tools cut best in most
applications with the bevel rubbing
or very close. So, if you are trying
out a new tool or find that you are
having trouble using a tool, go back
to basics and rub the bevel on the
work, gradually moving the tool so
that the edge starts to produce fine
shavings; then push the tool along
or into the wood at that angle. Also,
when trying a new tool or new
technique, hold the tool against the

Fig. 9
Chucks: (*top left*) Axminster four-jaw
127 mm (5 in), (*bottom left*) Pratt Burnard
three-jaw 102 mm (4 in) (*centre*) shop-
made hornbeam cup chuck and (*bottom
right*) 12.5 mm ($\frac{1}{2}$ in) capacity Jacob's chuck

wood before starting the lathe so that you can see at what angles you can hold the tool such that the bevel rubs, and then rotate the wood by hand to see if it produces shavings. Start with the lathe at a slow speed until you are confident and then a faster speed when you are ready. There are no hard and fast rules about lathe speed but for each project I give the speed or range of speeds at which I set the lathe.

There is no reason why you should use your stronger hand on the rest or the end of the handle since both hands work just as hard.

There will be occasions when it is easier to approach the work using one hand rather than the other so it is best to practise using both hands at the rest.

If you are trying a new technique it makes a lot of sense to practise on a piece of cheap unseasoned wood so that you get the technique right before using a piece of expensive wood that you might waste. After all, you would not expect to write a book without first learning to write each individual letter.

Fundamental to a proper use of tools is an understanding of the way

that the structure of the wood affects the way it must be cut. The short answer is to cut 'downhill' which, in the case of all but one of the projects, is towards the axis of the lathe.

The reason for this is that wood can be loosely described as a bundle of fibres and the only way to cut it cleanly is to do so in a direction that means that the fibres you are cutting are supported by the fibres underneath. You would not sharpen a pencil from the lead outwards so it does not make sense to turn in this direction.

CHUCKS

Where you need to hollow one end of a piece of work, as in the case of bowls and boxes, you need to support the other end by means of a chuck. There are very many chucks available now and it is very difficult to decide which one to buy. The ones I use are in **fig. 9** and are: top left, Axminster four-jaw 127 mm (5 in), bottom left, Pratt Burnard three-jaw 102 mm (4 in), centre, shop made hornbeam cup chuck, top right, Craft Supplies Collet chuck and bottom right, 12.5 mm ($\frac{1}{2}$ in) capacity Jacob's chuck.

I introduce these chucks when used in the projects but it should be said that chucks with projecting jaws can injure the careless user either by catching the knuckles or when the chuck key is left in place when the lathe starts up. The best way to avoid the latter happening is to get into the habit of never leaving the chuck key in the chuck when not using it while the only way to avoid the former is to be constantly aware of the danger. I think that these chucks are so useful and versatile that it is worth the extra care needed when using them.

ABRASIVES

Garnet paper is the cheapest type of abrasive I would recommend, but the grits do tend to detach from the paper when it is damp or where it is folded. Once the grits get into the wood there is no way you can use the tools again without blunting them. However, if you do use garnet paper I recommend that you use the lightest papers because are the most flexible when papering around curves.

The best abrasives are coated, cloth-backed aluminium oxide where the grits do not have the same tendency to become loose. The abrasives also cut more efficiently than garnet and leave a smoother finish. Though initially more expensive than garnet, since they last a lot longer they work out cheaper.

A useful selection of grits to have is 80, 100, 180 and 240. When you have got as good a finish from the tool as possible you start with the lowest number and only when you have removed all the bits of rough grain do you progress to the next grade. When you have got rid of the marks left by the previous grades you can progress to the next finer grade. If you keep the abrasive moving all the time you should avoid making very deep grooves, and if you fold the abrasive in three you will protect your fingers from getting too hot. It is best to hold the abrasive so that if it catches on the work it will be pulled out of your hand not pushed into it (see **fig. 24**, page 34). As you can see in fig. 24 you should always remove the rest when sanding to prevent the fingers from being trapped between the rest and the work.

Abrasives can alter the shape of what you have turned but you should only do this consciously. To avoid accidentally blurring your nice fine detailing you should cut the abrasive into small strips and only sand one face at a time. Too much sanding not only spoils the sharpness of some detail but can also change the cross section from circular to oval which can be a big fault in certain cases. This effect is called differential sanding and is caused by some parts of the wood being more easily eroded than others.

SAFETY FIRST

The workshop is a potentially dangerous place because of the presence of electricity, sharp-edged tools and machines capable of rotating large lumps of wood at high speeds. The best way to handle these dangers is to keep your workshop tidy and well organized. Most safety rules are common sense, but that sense can be put to the back of the mind when the creative urge is driving you.

There are two periods in their career when the turner is particularly prone to self-inflicted damage: the first is when unfamiliarity with tools and processes leads to mistakes and the second is when familiarity has bred contempt. After you have a nasty and painful experience with a tool you tend to associate it with pain and thereafter be careful. The time of day when you are most likely to have an accident is in the afternoon when most of us feel tired for an hour or two. If your attention is wandering and you find yourself thinking of something other than what you are doing it is time to have a break.

Perhaps the worst hazard is the least obvious and that is dust. It is easy to ignore this until you find that your lungs or sinuses have suffered irrevocable damage. In Britain and the States you have a statutory duty to control this hazard, and it is in your best interest to use an efficient personal air filter and a dust extractor.

The lathe itself is potentially dangerous because the wood can detach itself and become an unguided missile. Here are some strategies to minimize this risk:

- Double check that the wood is firmly held on the lathe.

- Where possible, avoid standing to the side of work held at only one end (such as on a faceplate) as this is the direction it is most likely to fly.

- Always turn the wood by hand before starting the lathe to see that nothing will snag it.

- Check the speed before you turn it on (it is a good idea to leave the lathe set at a slow speed so that if you forget to check there should be no danger).

- Keep a line of retreat open so that you can run away from a potential disaster while you think what to do about it.

- Always wear some sort of eye protection.

COSTING WORK

Most people get their biggest buzz when someone likes a piece of work enough to pay for it, but how do you decide on the price? You will probably increase the likelihood of selling if you do not charge much and perhaps just make enough to cover the cost of the wood – but this has some knock-on effects that I would like you to consider. The most immediate effect is that when you have to replace a tool, buy some more abrasive, or repair a piece of machinery the money will have to come from some source other than sales. But there are other more long-term results, for the effect of selling cheaply reduces the value the buying public places upon woodturnery and this in turn affects the sales of the professional quite apart from the fact that it represents subsidized competition. I have heard of low prices being justified by a low standard of work but this is a terrible argument because you should only sell work of which you are proud – apart from the fact that selling poor quality work further lowers the public opinion of our craft. In order to work out the correct wholesale price for a piece of work you need three figures:

- The cost per hour of running your workshop.

- The cost of the raw material.

- The amount you want to earn per hour.

To work out a figure to represent the cost of each hour you spend at the lathe you need to add up the rent for the workshop, insurance of the building and contents, electricity, part of the cost of the car according to how much you use it

for woodturning such as buying wood, tools, attending exhibitions of machinery, demonstrations, selling events etc. You should also include amounts spent on raw materials such as finishes and abrasives which are difficult to apportion to particular items, and an amount to cover the cost of depreciation of machinery and the cost of repairing it. You divide the totals of all of these plus any others you can think of by the number of hours you spend per year turning and with this hourly rate you can see how much it costs you to stand in the workshop even when you are not producing (see **fig. 10**).

The cost of the wood is calculated by working out the cubic volume of the blank you start with i.e. length × breadth × thickness, and dividing this number (so many cubic mm or inches) into the number of cubic mm or inches that make up the basic unit you bought, such as per cubic metre or cubic feet.

This gives you a number you would theoretically get from a cubic unit and if you divide this number into the price per cubic unit you have the cost of the wood which you should then double to take account of wastage and time spent choosing, fetching and converting.

These two figures need to be added to the amount you want to earn per hour to give you a rough idea of the final price. You might say that you do not need to earn any money if your interest is purely recreational, but if you sell your produce then your interest is already more than just recreational and it will give you an idea of how the professional arrives at his prices.

To cover all the costs involved the professional ought to add in factors for time spent designing and doing the books but these are often ignored for fear of driving the price through the roof.

This is how the wholesale price is worked out. If your work is sold in a shop they will put a mark up on your price to cover their costs which include staff wages, rent, insurance, heating advertising and so on. This will very often double the wholesale price and if a professional sells his work directly to a customer the same sort of mark up should apply because while the selling process is going on production time is lost. If the selling takes place at a craft fair the mark up also has to cover travel costs and paying for the stall.

DESIGN CRITERIA

In each project I have included a paragraph or two on this subject. I have not gone into great detail about the theories that have been put forward to explain why certain things are more pleasing to the majority of people (such as the Golden Section of Euclid and the Fibonacci Series) because I think that their interest lies in explanation rather than in design. If you design objects using mathematical formulae you deny the individual input that separates the well-made craft item from the mass-produced. As a subject I find design theory fascinating and it may help you to approach designing in a more rational way if you understand why some shapes work, so I have included some books on the subject in my list of recommended reading and I discuss this subject in *Turning Bowls: Step-by-Step*.

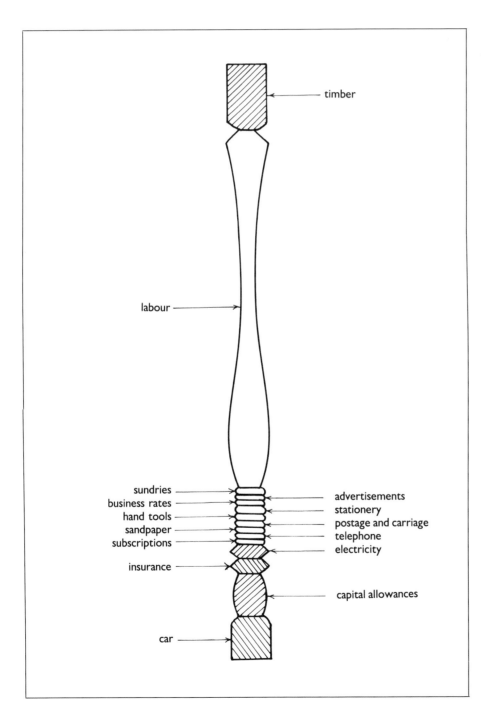

Fig. 10

Breakdown of components of *wholesale* price for typical turned item (to convert to retail price multiply by two)

– PART TWO

PROJECTS

PESTLE AND MORTAR

DESIGN CRITERIA

Pestles and mortars are used to grind up either spices or garlic for cooking or tablets and coarse crystals into powders in cooking or medicine (**fig. 11**). The wood should therefore be hard, not very porous, odourless, washable and not poisonous. The finish should not contain chemicals that may be harmful and should not be of the varnish type that forms a film on the surface because this will be worn away. Cooking oil or medicinal liquid paraffin are ideal, with a thin waxing of beeswax for appearance sake if required.

As you can see from **fig. 12** the shape of the business end of the pestle should be designed with the shape of the inside of the mortar in mind. The two surfaces should be able to crush the substance concerned, in other words there should be no sudden dips in the

Fig. 11
Pestle and mortar 100 mm (4 in) across and 50 mm (2 in) deep in olive ash

Fig. 12
Cross section of pestle and mortar
showing how the pestle fits the mortar

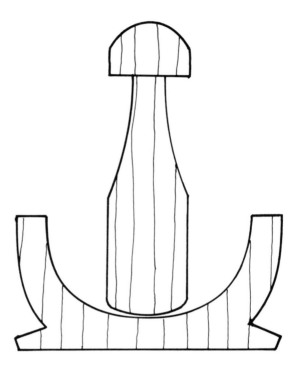

mortar that the pestle cannot reach. The grinding end of the pestle should be smaller than the inside of the mortar to give room for the grist but there is plenty of margin for personal taste on this point. The inside of the mortar should be deep enough to hold the contents without them spilling out while being ground and the sides should be steep so that the bits that have not been ground return to the bottom to receive the attentions of the pestle. It is useful for the user to be able to grip the base of the mortar while grinding so I always include a foot in my designs and I make the base as wide as possible for stability. The sides and bottom of the mortar should be quite thick to withstand the pressure of the pestle and the pestle should be comfortable to hold in the palm of the hand.

DIRECTION OF GRAIN

The grain of the wood for the pestle should run from end to end because the strength of wood is along its length and because it is harder to turn spindles with the grain running across. The direction of the grain in the mortar should ideally run from top to bottom because wood is harder and wears more evenly on the end of the grain than on the side (that is why traditional, beechwood, butchers' chopping blocks are made with the end grain on the surface). A section across the grain reveals a closely bunched bundle of tube ends which are uniformly hard and wear more evenly than the sides of the tubes as revealed by a section along the grain. When the sides of the grain are abraded the soft parts are worn away and the harder parts are

left as ridges. These rings are caused by differences of cell type and rate of growth in response to different seasons and different growing conditions. Because some are harder than others and are aligned as they are, the softer parts are worn away more quickly and the harder parts are left as ridges.

I have made mortars for sale as small as 25 mm (1 in) across but the size that sells most readily is 100 mm (4 in) across and 50 mm (2 in) deep. These need seasoned timber 100 mm thick to be turned with the grain running from top to bottom and this is not easy to obtain. I use off-cuts from bowl blanks which I leave to season in billets 100 × 100 mm with the end-grain sealed by emulsified paraffin wax (End-grain sealer or Mobilcer C). The length of time these take to dry depends on their original water content and the conditions in which they are kept, but it can take four years (you generally reckon on one year for each inch of thickness). Therefore, if you cannot wait and cannot obtain dry timber 100 mm thick you can turn them with the grain running from side to side out of timber 50 mm (2 in) thick which is easier to find. Only if the mortar is used a great deal will differential wear result.

The techniques needed to make a mortar with the grain running this way are basic bowl-turning techniques, but if you make a mortar with the grain running from top to bottom the grain dictates the use of a quite different method which I will describe at length because it is used in many of the projects in this book. I shall also describe the turning of the pestle in detail because this also involves the use of some basic techniques which will be used for other projects in this book.

margin for error and a bit at both ends (spigot) which will be marked by the centres.

Mounting the blank

The fork centre which does the driving is 18.75 mm ($\frac{3}{4}$ in) across, and this is preferable to a larger one which you can more easily catch with the tool when turning something as small as this. I do not mark the centre of the blank when turning a piece this size as it is easy, with a bit of practice, to judge the centre by eye. The trick, when centring at the headstock, is to hold the wood up to the centre looking from one face, and if the gap between the ends of the dogs and the sides are equal you hold the wood against the centre and rotate it to see if it is also central between the other sides (**fig. 13**). To centre the wood accurately at the tailstock

end is not so easy because you only have a point there and the distance from that to the faces of the blank is further and not so easy to judge by eye. If this is a problem you can mark the centre of one end using the fork centre and then reverse the wood and use this centre mark at the tailstock end. If you have difficulty with this method, diagonals drawn on the ends will meet sufficiently near the centre for a job of this nature even if the sides of the blank are not absolutely square.

Fig. 13

Centring pestle blank showing eventual shape of pestle and how it is easier to centralize it on the fork centre than on the tailstock centre

MAKING A PESTLE

- ☐ *Blank*: 37 mm ($1\frac{1}{2}$in) × 37 mm ($1\frac{1}{2}$in) × 137 mm ($5\frac{1}{2}$in).
- ☐ *Timber*: close-grained, odourless, non-poisonous e.g. ash, fruitwoods, sycamore, hornbeam; olive ash illustrated.
- ☐ *Tools*: basic kit.
- ☐ *Lathe speed I use*: 2250 rpm.

For a 100 mm (4 in) wide mortar I make a pestle 110 mm ($4\frac{1}{2}$ in) long and 31 m ($1\frac{1}{4}$ in) thick. The suggested blank allows you a

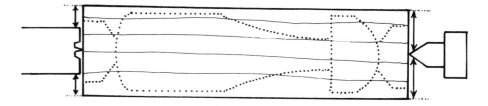

Before you start turning you ought to check that the speed of the lathe is appropriate. Remember, it is best to start slow and increase the speed as you become more proficient, and always rotate the work by hand before you start, to make sure that the work will rotate without snagging the rest.

Step one – roughing out

The square-section stock can be rounded using the roughing gouge moving from side to side with the flute facing in the direction of cut. As you can see from **fig. 14** the first cuts while the corners of the blank are still sharp should be done fairly gently with the centre of the cutting edge so that the corners of the gouge do not get anywhere near the wood. As the corners of the work are removed and the tool becomes easier to control the tool can be rolled over so that cuts are done with the tool more on its side as in **fig. 15**. You should develop a smooth, side to side action for this operation, rolling the tool over as you approach each extremity of the work so that the flute faces the direction of cut and the handle is about 70° to the axis of the lathe by the time you reach each end ready to return in the other direction. The secret of this motion is threefold.

- Support the handle end on the side of your body or hip (depending on your height relative to the lathe).

- Hold the tool at this point with a grip such that in order to rotate the tool you do not need to change your hand position but merely roll the wrist over.

Fig. 14
Pestle – roughing gouge and square stock, cutting with centre of edge

Fig. 15
Roughing gouge and round stock, cutting with side of tool

- Start at, for instance, the right end of the work with your weight on your right foot and your legs apart so that as you progress to the left you gradually transfer your weight to the left foot so that you do not have to move your feet.

The hand at the rest can be either the right or left (I suggest that you alternate), and the grip is not too critical except that you must make sure that part of your hand is in contact with the rest and none of your fingers get between the work and the rest.

Step two – sizing

When the blank has been rounded you need to establish the required diameter. The most flexible system for doing this is as illustrated in **fig. 16** i.e. with external callipers. For repetition work the use of a spanner of the required thickness is better because it does not need to be set to the correct dimension and will not alter during use as may a pair of callipers. See the section on scoops for more detail on the use of spanners (page 59). The callipers are set to the correct gap and the beading and parting tool is used to turn the work to that size. If you do this sizing at each end of the work you will be able to turn the whole cylinder to that thickness by eye, and, should you make a mistake and take off too much you will not have strayed onto the part of the blank that the pestle will come from.

The first few times you try this you may prefer to use the parting tool in both hands and stop the lathe before checking the thickness, but as you gain in skill you can use the callipers and the tool as in **fig. 16**. You must be careful not to press the callipers too hard onto the work as they will catch and either get bent or fly out of control. The only precaution you need take is to wear a face shield for they are not very heavy objects.

The action of the parting tool in this cut is described in the introduction (see **fig. 2**, page 13) i.e. up-and-over. This is the only way to cut with the support of the bevel, as pushing the tool straight in will cause a catch at worse and rapid wear of the tool at best.

When the blank is the right diameter you can mark the length by means of dividers (**fig. 17**). If you

Fig. 16

Sizing thickness with external callipers

hold them lightly and press gently you will be less likely to get a catch and if you do get one the dividers will tend to fly away from you. However, it is always worth putting on a face shield just in case. Do not forget to sharpen the dividers like any other tool. This should be done with a bevel on the outside so that the point is in line with the straight, inner edge.

Step three – spigots

The waste at either end of the work enables you to turn a spigot so that if you should lose control of the tool near the ends you will have a safety margin before you hit the centres, which have an unfortunate tendency to blunt the tool rather quickly. You can turn down the spigot using the beading and parting

Fig. 17
Marking length with dividers pressing lightly

tool but if you can use a skew for the whole of the rest of the turning it is more efficient to use the skew for this as well. As you can see in **fig. 18**, this is a peeling cut with the skew on its side and its point on the pestle side of the cut at each end, so that you get a straight edge to correspond with the marks made by the dividers. As with the beading and parting tool the action is up-and-over so that the bevel supports the edge.

You should aim to leave the spigot just thick enough to support the work so that you can shape as much of the pestle as possible while it is still on the lathe, as it always seems to take an inordinate length of time to finish off the ends of a spindle after it has been parted off.

Fig. 18
Turning spigot with skew, peeling cut with the point on the divider's mark

Fig. 19
Rounding left end with rolling motion of skew

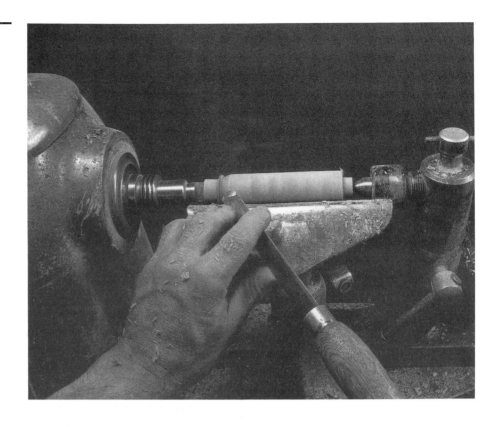

Fig. 20
Rounding left end using other hand at rest

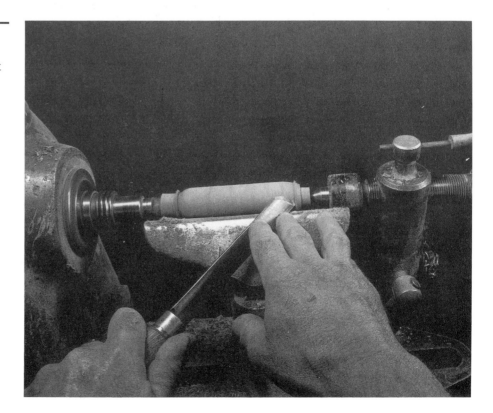

Step four – shaping

After forming the spigots, the ends of the pestle need to be rounded using a rolling motion of the skew (**figs. 19–20**). I prefer to do this with the point (the toe) first because I can see it more clearly than the heel, which tends to be obscured by the body of the skew. If you use the point for the first cuts you can remove wood at quite a fast rate but as you get close to the shape you require you can do a more gentle cut with the part of the edge just down from the point (the paring cut, see **fig. 4**, page 15).

The stem of the pestle is a sort of cove so you start by making a vee cut with the point and gradually enlarging one side of it to form the stem and the other to form the bottom edge of the knob as near to a right angle as suits your taste (**figs. 21–23**).

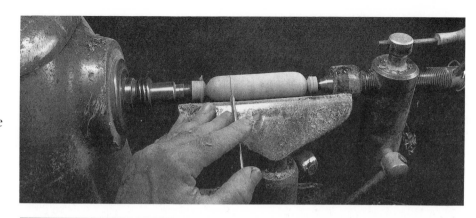

Fig. 21
Starting vee cut with skew at right angles to axis

Fig. 22
Widening vee cut from the right, cutting with point first

Fig. 23
Forming stem with skew right over on its side

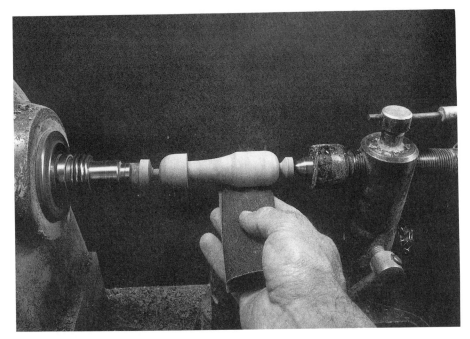

Fig. 24
Sanding – abrasive held so rotation pulls it away from fingers. Note the rest removed for safety

Step five – finishing

The finish from the tool should be good enough to require little sanding but if the grain is unruly you might have to use 100 grit, then 180 and finally 220 (**fig. 24**). For the finish I use a cooking oil which is applied with the wood stationary and then beeswax while the wood is rotating. I buff this with a rag.

Fig. 25
Parting off, ready to catch the pestle when it breaks loose

Step six – parting off

I part off the pestle with the skew so that I can leave a good finish on the ends which will then require little subsequent finishing. The final cuts are done with the work supported with one hand and the tool held in the other as in **fig. 25** so that you can catch the pestle as it breaks free. You should do the end at the tailstock first because the rotational force is applied from the headstock end and you need to leave this part as thick as possible for as long as possible. The trick is to judge just how little you can leave at the tailstock end so that your parting off cut at the headstock end can proceed without breaking off the other end.

MAKING A MORTAR

- *Blank*: 100 mm (4 in) × 100 mm (4 in) × 187 mm (7½ in)
- *Timber*: as pestle.
- *Tools*: Basic kit, plus; four-jaw, self-centring chuck (Axminster) or cup chuck, 6.25 mm (¼ in) spindle gouge, 37.5 mm (1½ in) half round scraper, hammer or mallet.
- *Lathe speed I use*: 1330 rpm.

Step one – mounting

To make a mortar you obviously have to support the blank at one end so that you can hollow out the other. With the grain running from top to bottom you cannot use a faceplate and screws because screws do not hold well in end grain. It is also not a good idea to use an expanding chuck as this could split the wood because of the way the grain is running. You will save wood and time if you prepare a 100 mm (4 in) × 100 mm (4 in) × 187 mm (7.5 in) blank so that once you have mounted the blank you can make several mortars or other similar items without removing the wood from the lathe.

If you have a four-jaw, self-centring chuck you can mount the wood in that. If you do not have such a tool and only have a faceplate you will need to make a cup chuck as in the small end-grain bowl project pages. In the photos I am using a 125 mm (5 in) chuck but a 100 mm (4 in) chuck is adequate for most purposes.

If the sides of the blank and the end are square it can be mounted in the four-jaw without further ado,

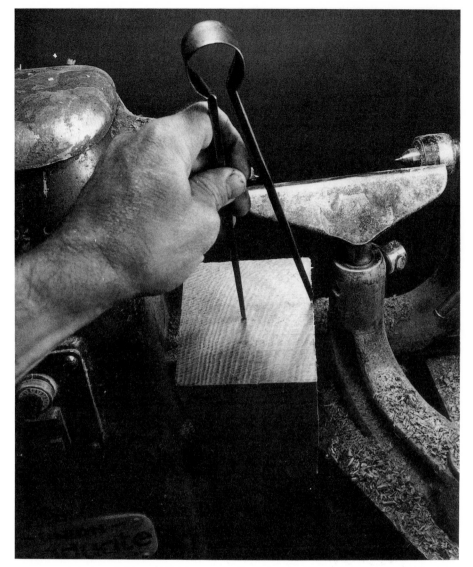

but if not it must be turned true between centres because it will be more stable in the jaws if the end fits flush against the chuck. First, you need to mark the centres accurately at each end. If the sides are square this can be done by drawing diagonal lines which naturally meet at the centre. However, if you dry your own blanks, as I do, the sides will be distorted and the diagonals will not meet at the centre. In this case you can set dividers at the radius and locate the centre by eye as in **fig. 26**, checking that it is

Fig. 26
Mortar – finding centre of end with dividers in case blank is distorted

correct by describing a circle which should touch two opposite faces and be equidistant from the other two.

The blank is rounded with the roughing gouge and the tailstock end trued up with the beading and parting tool, skew or fluted parting tool as in **fig. 27**.

Fig. 27
Truing end with fluted parting tool

Fig. 28
Smoothing end with skew, slicing cut, note how tool's angle makes bevel's angle subtend 90 degrees with axis

Using such a chuck can be dangerous if you are not conscious at all times of the fact that the projecting jaws can do you a nasty injury. There are several ways of avoiding damage such as covering the jaws with a piece of motorcycle inner tubing or painting the jaws a bright colour. I do none of these because I believe that since what I am doing is potentially dangerous at all times I cannot afford to forget this about any operation. One thing I do as a matter of routine is not to leave the chuck key in the socket when I am not holding it because it becomes an unguided missile if left in when the lathe is started.

Step two – roughing out

Use roughing gouge as on page 28 and then true up the end using the skew slicing cut as in **fig. 28**.

Step three – sizing

If you want to do a run of mortars, all of the same diameter, then you will have to use callipers to establish this as with the pestle (page 29), but if you are not too concerned about the size do not bother. The external height of the mortar can be marked out with dividers and the fluted parting tool used to establish it, making sure that you leave enough of a spigot to support the mortar while turning.

Step four – shaping

The outside shape is turned with a skew using the techniques described in the making of the pestle (**fig. 29**).

Fig. 29
Outside shape of mortar showing size of spigot and enough wood for two more mortars

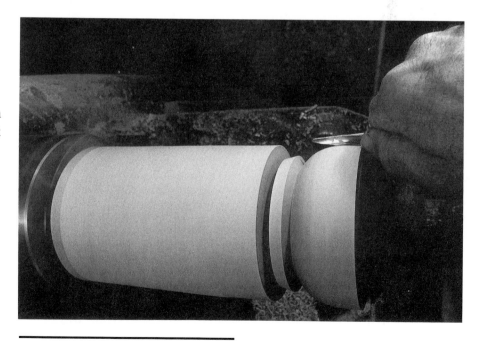

Fig. 30
Measuring depth holding gouge on outside and marking depth with thumb

Step five – marking inside depth

The first job is to establish the depth of the mortar using the 6.25 mm (¼ in) spindle gouge that will be doing the hollowing. If you cut a funnel-shape first, the steam created by the depth cut will expand before burning your fingers. You can then do a straight cut into the mortar for a short distance before holding the gouge along the outside of the mortar to see how deep you want it to be (**fig. 30**). Using your thumb as a marker, insert the gouge into the central hole of the mortar and press it in until your thumb is level with the top.

Step six – hollowing with gouge

The gouge is then inserted into the hole a short distance and pulled outwards cutting as it comes (**fig. 31**). The part of the edge that does the cutting is back from the point, and if the tool handle lies along the forearm and the thumb is on top of the tool (a short distance back from the point) there is not a lot of work for the other hand to do (**fig. 32**).

The rest is positioned so that the tool tip points upward to cut the centre of the bottom of the mortar but the bevel does not rub during this cut (**fig. 33**). You will find that you can remove the timber at a fast rate but it is also easy to lose control if you do not go steadily and surely and keep the rest close to the work. As you progress with the hollowing you may find that you need to move the rest inside the bowl. I have a rest which comes to a sharp point which I can use to get into narrow openings such as this and the goblet (see page 54).

There are other methods of hollowing end grain one of which is described in Holtzapffel's book and another in Richard Raffan's *Turning wood*. I have tried both of these with no success but if you fail with my method you may have better success with theirs. The main point to remember is that because the

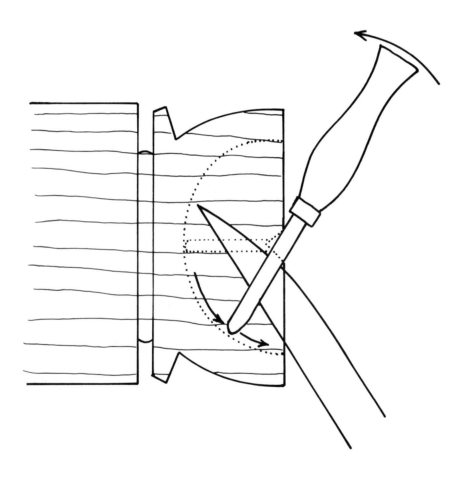

Fig. 31
Hollowing mortar with spindle gouge

Fig. 32
Hollowing, note how tool handle is well
supported by forearm

Fig. 33
Hollowing, see how the bevel is not
rubbing in this cut

Fig. 34
Finish from gouge is quite good

Fig. 35
Smoothing cut with scraper with the rest below centre height and tool pointing up

Fig. 36
Finish from scraper which removes the little ridges left by the gouge

grain is running along the axis you must use a different method than when the grain is running at right angles to the axis. As in all woodworking it is the grain that dictates the best way for it to be cut.

Step seven – finish with scraper

Fig. 34 shows the finish that can be obtained from the gouge. It looks fairly good but it can be improved by a few gentle passes of the 37.5 mm ($1\frac{1}{2}$ in) half round scraper which must cut the centre (**fig. 35**) or you will leave a dome there. Traditionally this tool is used with the rest above centre height and

pointing downwards. You can get a cleaner, shearing cut, however, with it pointing upwards, provided that you go gently and make sure that if you tilt the tool on the rest, the side of the tool doing the cutting is the side of the tool on the rest. Because of the grain direction the best way for this cut to be made is from the centre outwards. **Fig. 36** shows the finish from the scraper.

Step eight – finish (see page 34)

The mortar is then ready to be sanded and the finish of edible oil and wax to be applied as on the pestle.

Step nine – parting off

Parting off can be done with the fluted parting tool using the left hand to hold the mortar not the tool (**fig. 37**).

Step ten – finishing bottom

Parting off with the above method leaves a fairly rough bottom which can be turned smooth by holding the outside of the mortar in the external jaws of the four-jaw chuck, provided that you protect the work with a piece of cloth (**fig. 38**). If you have been using a cup chuck you can remount the mortar on the remainder of the wood in the

Fig. 37
Parting off with the left hand ready to catch
the mortar

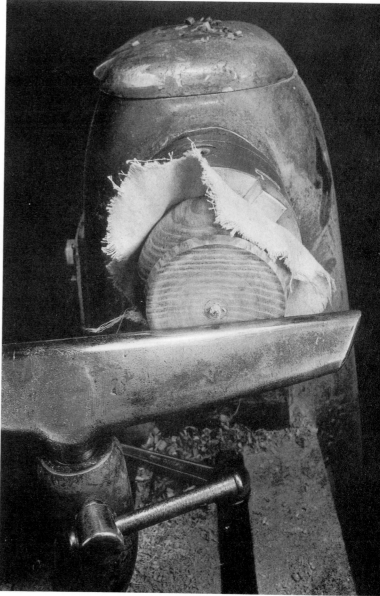

Fig. 38
Remounted in four-jaw chuck with cloth
protecting wood

Fig. 39
Removing knob with 6.25 mm ($\frac{1}{4}$ in) bowl gouge cutting inwards

Fig. 40
Smoothing end with side of bowl gouge working inwards

Fig. 41
Finish from gouge before the use of abrasives

chuck as for the small bowl (see **figs. 47–51**).

I finish off the bottoms of mortars in two steps with a 6.25 mm ($\frac{1}{4}$ in), ground-back, bowl gouge: first working towards the centre with the flute pointing in the direction of cut to remove the knob (**fig. 39**); and then doing a smoothing cut with the side of the gouge, working from the centre outwards (**fig. 40**). **Fig. 41** shows the finish from the gouge, before the use of abrasives.

−2−

SMALL END-GRAIN BOWL

DESIGN CRITERIA

If you can obtain seasoned timber
100 mm (4 in) or 75 mm (3 in)
square in lengths of 150 mm (6 in)
and upwards you can make stacks of
bowls using the same techniques as
for mortars. This is a lot more
efficient than individually chucking
each one. The bowls are useful for
serving a catholic assortment of
substances such as salt, sugar or
even peanuts and the design
requirements are correspondingly
less stringent than for the mortar.
The sides can be quite thin, say
2 mm ($\frac{1}{8}$ in) because they do not
need to be very strong and the base
does not have to be very wide. I
make the bases of this type of bowl
quite small, because I think it looks
good. At first glance they might
look unstable but if you tilt them
they tend to right themselves,
particularly if they have contents as
these lower the centre of gravity.

Fig. 42
Small bowl, 100 mm (4 in) across × 50 mm
(2 in) deep in olive ash

43

MAKING A SMALL END-GRAIN BOWL

☐ *Blank*: 75 mm (3 in) × 75 mm (3 in) × 175 mm (7 in) illustrated, but could be larger or smaller.
☐ *Timber*: any straight-grained hardwood.
☐ *Tools*: basic tool kit plus 6.25 mm ($\frac{1}{4}$ in) spindle gouge and one-sided skew, four-jaw or cup chuck.
☐ *Lathe speed I use*: 1330 rpm.

Step one – mounting

If you have not got a four-jaw chuck and all you possess is a faceplate you can make yourself a cup chuck to mount this type of work. I made the one in the photo of this project approximately 12 years ago because I could not afford the metal one made for the lathe and it has given me sterling service. I used hornbeam which is the most suitable, readily available, locally grown timber for the job but also suitable would be one of the fruit woods or *Robinia pseudoacacia*. It is 150 mm (6 in) diameter and 50 mm (2 in) thick and is held onto the faceplate with four 37.5 mm (1$\frac{1}{2}$ in) no. 14 screws. The hole goes all the way through so that the wood held in it can be released by driving a rod through the hollow headstock; it is also slightly tapered so that as the wood is driven into it, it is compressed.

Mount the blank between centres and form the spigot on the end with the beading and parting tool, using callipers as in making the pestle. You should make the diameter of the tailstock end of the spigot equal to the diameter of the hole in the cup chuck at its opening, so that as you drive the spigot in it is compressed. The spigot is formed at the tailstock end (**fig. 43**) because you will do less damage to the tool if you slip and hit the rotating centre than if you hit the driving centre.

Fig. 43
Blank with spigot which is slightly tapered

The wood can be driven into the chuck off the lathe as in **fig. 44**, and if the shoulder of the blank ends up flush with the top of the chuck, it should be centred when mounted on the lathe. If, and only if, you have really strong bearings on your lathe, you can drive the wood in while it is on the lathe and by rotating it while hitting it can make sure that it is centred. If it goes off centre you must not correct it by striking the side of the blank as this will tend to push it out of the chuck, but rather you must strike it on the end to one side or the other depending on which way it needs to go.

Steps two to five

Roughing out, sizing, shaping outside, and marking depth are carried out as for the mortar.

Step six – hollowing with gouge

The use of the tool is the same as in step six of the mortar project on page 38, but because the sides of the bowl are thinner than the sides of the mortar you will find that as you approach the required thickness the tool will begin to chatter. This is because the sides are flexible enough to distort away from the tool. Obviously you will not get a satisfactory finish if this is going on so the remedy is to absorb the vibrations with the hand not holding the tool (**fig. 45**). The fact that the handle of the tool is along the forearm, as in **fig. 32**, page 39 (mortar), means that you only need to have the thumb of the hand at

Fig. 44
Mounting blank in cup chuck by hitting it with a mallet

Fig. 45
Hollowing with spindle gouge using left
hand to absorb vibrations

the rest on top of the tool to steady
it and the rest of the fingers are
available to press on the outside of
the bowl. The pressure applied by
the fingers is a matter of experience
but if you can smell burning flesh
and your fingers are feeling hot I
suggest that you should not be
pressing quite so hard.

Step seven – finish with scraper

(see page 40)

Step eight – finishing

(see page 34)

Step nine – parting off

This can be done with the fluted
parting tool but a better finish on
the bottom can be obtained with a
skew, and this means that there will
be less finishing off to do afterwards.
Unfortunately, because a skew has
two bevels, you can only use it on
the bottom by making the gap
between the base of the bowl and
the next one inordinately wide. I
have got around this problem by
sharpening a skew so that it only
has one bevel. This means that the
bottom of the bowl can be turned
with a slight concavity and if you
judge it just right, it needs no
further finishing and no larger gap
than that needed for the fluted
parting tool. The cut is done as in
fig. 46 with the bevel facing the left
and the cutting done with the point.

This cut requires the very greatest
care for if you allow the tool to
rotate very slightly to the right, the
edge as well as the point comes into

contact with the base of the bowl and a catch results; there is even less margin for error on this tool than the ordinary skew!

When you get to the point where the bowl is about to break free you can support it in the spare hand as in the mortar. At this point, if the bottom of the bowl is thin and you are too heavy handed, you can end up with a spigot on the blank and a bowl with a hole in the bottom. This occurs because the only point of contact between the bowl and the lathe, i.e. the point that is driving the bowl, is that small spigot and there tends to be insufficient strength across the grain to overcome the inertia of the bowl. To avoid this happening, you must not grip the bowl too tightly because this can cause it to stop rotating when it ought to be still joined to the spigot; rather, you should aim to leave a small knob on the base of the bowl rather than cut too close to the bottom as this gives more strength to the spigot. If you then pare away at the part of the spigot nearest to the blank it will tend to break off at this point rather than pull a plug out of the bottom.

Step ten – finishing bottom

When you get very proficient with the one-sided skew you will find that you need do little finishing on the bottom; but until you reach this stage, you will need to reverse chuck it as with the mortar. Should you not have a four-jaw chuck to do this you can cut a spigot on the end of the blank to push the bowl onto. This is a useful technique used a lot in the making of boxes and requires only care and patience.

Fig. 46
Parting off with one-sided skew, bevel facing left to cut square with point, which has no bevel

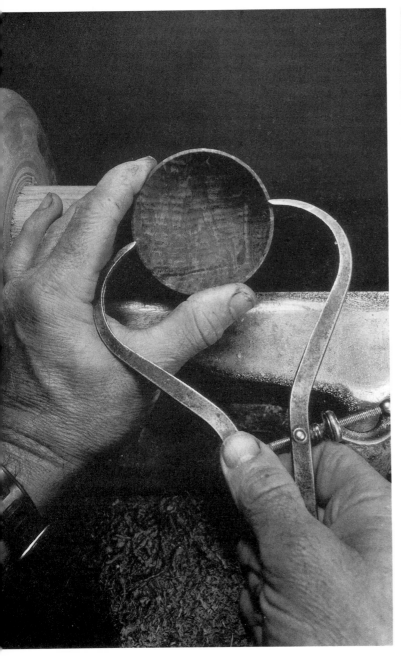

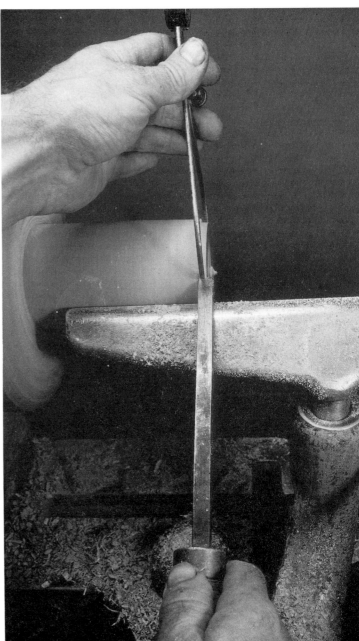

Fig. 47
Measuring inside diameter using external callipers

Fig. 48
Forming short spigot using beading and parting tool and measuring with external callipers

You need to measure the inside diameter of the bowl with external callipers (**fig. 47**) and then make a very short spigot on the end of the blank with the beading and parting tool, as when sizing the pestle (**fig. 48**). If you make a very short spigot and then see if the bowl fits onto it, you will not have lost much wood if you made the first cut too deep and you need to make another spigot. For your first attempt at this technique I suggest that you stop the lathe to see if the bowl fits, but eventually you should be able to check this with the blank still rotating.

If the bowl fits snugly on the spigot, it can be lengthened with a skew (**fig. 49**) to give the bowl adequate support – 6 mm ($\frac{1}{4}$ in) should be enough. The spigot should be tapered slightly so that the fit gets tighter as the bowl is pressed on (**figs. 50–51**). It is a mistake to make the taper too steep because the bowl then becomes difficult to centre, and it might also result in the bowl splitting if it is forced on too vigorously. The aim is to make it just tight enough to enable you to finish the bottom and not so tight that you have to lever it off with the possibility of damaging the top. It is a good idea to put a grid in front of the dust extractor while doing a batch of bottoms as the effect of a fan blade on a small bowl is rather more than textural. Should the fit on the spigot be slightly too loose you can put a piece of cloth or tissue over it to make it snug.

I finish bottoms with a 6.25 mm ($\frac{1}{4}$ in) ground-back gouge (as on page 42) before sanding.

Fig. 49
Lengthening spigot with skew when fit has been confirmed

Fig. 50
Bowl mounted on spigot

Fig. 51
Bottom of bowl to be finished

-3-

GOBLET

DESIGN CRITERIA

First, a word of warning: the one thing that wooden goblets are not good for is holding liquid. There are several other materials that are much better suited for the purpose such as glass and clay and I make very few goblets for this reason. I have, however, included one as a project (**fig. 52**) because some people like to make them and they are a step in the direction of making scoops. The problem with making a goblet in wood is inherent in its natural characteristics. You need the grain to run along the stem to maximize its natural strength and to avoid turning the stem with the grain running across, which is very difficult. As a result, the grain in the bowl runs from top to bottom, which means that the tubes from which the wood is made are in the best position to act as drains, quite the opposite of what is required.

Fig. 52

Goblet, 75 mm (3 in) × 75 mm (3 in) × 163 mm (6½ in), olive ash

Having said that, there are woods that are naturally less porous than average. The mazers (drinking vessels) in the Pinto collection are mostly made of *Lignum vitae*, one of the hardest woods known and particularly suitable for the purpose because of its natural oiliness. I would not recommend that anyone should have any part in the destruction of the rain forests so as far as I am concerned the use of *Lignum vitae* is no longer a viable option. I know of no timbers in temperate climes that are anywhere near as suitable. I believe that they would all either leak or crack if liquid were left in them unless they were treated with some kind of sealant, and although you can buy sealants that purport to be waterproof, I have not tried them myself.

To reduce the porosity of the wood in the bowl it is necessary to make the bottom thicker than the sides and, if you want to make the goblet look as if it could be drunk from, then a thin, but not sharp, rim is lip friendly. The base needs to be fairly wide and heavy to be stable and the stem needs to be fairly thick to be strong enough.

The above design criteria for a functional piece make it very difficult to make a goblet that I find aesthetically pleasing, which is another reason why I do not make many. If, however, you wish to make a goblet that has no functional aspirations then your design options are much greater. There are some traditional features of goblet design that you can discover by studying examples in museums or shops that specialize in glass ware. But remember that some features, such as a thin stem in a functional glass, are not so strong in a functional wooden goblet.

It is a good discipline to look at shapes with a critical eye and ask yourself if you like certain shapes and if so, why. Rough sketches will also force you to analyse shapes precisely. Often you will find that the stem and the bowl will be equal in length and that the profile of the bowl will echo (but not exactly copy) the profile of the stem. There is often a 'knop' (a knob) at the base of the bowl, which is there to punctuate the change in direction of the profile from the stem to the bowl, and frequently the diameter of the base is the same as the top of the bowl. These are all features you will see in the goblet I have made. Ask yourself if they work for you. Whatever you decide in terms of function and design the following method will enable you to make a goblet.

MAKING A GOBLET

- *Blank*: 75 mm (3 in) × 75 mm (3 in) × 185 mm (7½ in).
- *Timber*: for functional goblets see above, decorative ones whatever you like.
- *Tools*: basic kit plus four-jaw, self centring chuck (Axminster) or cup chuck, 6.25 mm (¼ in) spindle gouge, 37.5 mm (1½ in) half round scraper, hammer or mallet.
- *Lathe speed I use*: 1330 rpm.

Step one – mounting

See instructions on page 44.

Step two – roughing out

This is done with roughing gouge, as on page 28. **Fig. 53** shows how far you can go with the roughing gouge before you run the risk of contact with the jaws. At this stage it is advisable to complete the roughing out with the beading and parting tool which works at right angles to the axis and will not tend to slide towards the jaws, leaving the blank as in **fig. 54**. The end can now be trued up with the skew (**fig. 55**).

Step three – sizing

Only if you intend to make a matching set will you need to use callipers on the diameters. If you have worked out beforehand that you intend to do a specific shape, you will need to mark it out on the roughed blank with dividers. See Project 9 for more details about marking out (page 98).

Step four – shaping

The outside shaping is done with a roughing gouge and skew as on page 33, but you need to be especially careful at the base end if you are using a four-jaw chuck, as a catch could send your hand and chisel into the path of the jaws. The only part that needs shaping to the final dimensions at this stage is the bowl. The stem should not be done now as you need to leave sufficient wood there to support the bowl while hollowing it.

Fig. 53
Blank in four-jaw chuck, partly roughed out with roughing gouge

Fig. 54
Roughed blank in four-jaw chuck, roughing out process finished with beading and parting tool

Fig. 55
Smoothing end with skew

Fig. 56
Hollowing, showing tool handle along
forearm and tool rest inside bowl

Fig. 57
Hollowing, close up showing bevel not
rubbing and support of left hand outside
bowl

Step five – hollowing with gouge

The only difference between hollowing the goblet and the mortar is that the goblet bowl is deeper. This does not pose any great problems, provided that you can get your rest into the bowl so that the tip of the spindle gouge does not project too far over the rest. The nearer the support the less flexing the tool will do and the easier it is to get a smooth finish from the tool (**fig. 56**). As with the small bowl the thinness of the walls necessitates some support from the fingers of the left hand. **Fig. 57** shows that the bevel is not rubbing in this cut, so it requires great care.

Step six – finishing with scraper

This is much the same as in the mortar except that again the depth might cause a problem if the rest cannot go far enough into the bowl. This is worse than in ordinary bowls where the grain runs from side to side because the end grain in the bottom is more likely to catch the tool than side grain. The answer is to make sure that the tool is sharp, that the position of the rest enables the tool to be pointing down and that you only take off the thinnest of shavings. The sides of the bowl can be done with the tool pointing slightly upwards, but, as with the gouge, the support of the left hand on the outside is necessary to absorb the vibrations that cause the tool to judder (**fig. 58**).

Fig. 58
Smoothing cut with scraper with left hand supporting outside

55

Step seven – forming stem

This is done with the skew as usual, but as you can see from **fig. 59** the best way to keep clear of the chuck is to do it with the heel of the tool downwards. It is also a good idea to hold the tool with the grip shown to keep the fingers clear of the chuck.

Step eight – finish

Follow the instructions for sanding and applying oil and wax as on page 34.

Step nine – parting off

In **fig. 60** you can see that I parted off with a one sided skew as on page 46 so that the bottom was as smooth as possible when it came off the lathe.

Step ten – finishing bottom

This can be done by remounting the goblet in the external jaws of the chuck or on a spigot as on page 40, but because the goblet is longer than the mortar or the small bowl the support has to be firmer. I recommend, therefore, that the best way of re-chucking it is on a long spigot rather than in the jaws which, even if you protect the goblet with a piece of cloth, might mark the work if you have tighten them up a lot to give the necessary support.

Fig. 59
Forming stem with skew heel down

Fig. 60
Parting off with one-sided skew and fingers well out of way

−4−

Scoop

DESIGN CRITERIA

A scoop is used for shovelling up loose material (**fig. 61**). A small one might be used for fine grains such as salt or spices and a large one could be used for flour or porridge oats. Whatever the size, the essence of the scoop is that if you push it into a pile of material it should go in easily so that it can be filled up, and that once filled it should then hold its contents while they are carried to some receptacle where they will be deposited. For most normal people a common or garden spoon will do for most of these operations, although a cup might be harnessed for larger quantities. But being woodturners we have to be different.

The problem with making a scoop on the lathe is that it has to be symmetrical, and to be made quickly you have to be able to hollow out the business end without rechucking it. You cannot simply copy the ordinary spoon on the lathe because it is asymmetrical, but you can make what is in effect a cup on a handle and make it easier to push into loose material by removing some of the rim.

Fig. 61
Scoop, 38 mm ($1\frac{1}{2}$ in) × 38 mm ($1\frac{1}{2}$ in) × 113 mm ($4\frac{1}{2}$ in), olive ash

The cup has to be thin enough to push into the loose material and yet strong enough not to break under the strain of repeated use, while the handle has to be finger friendly and perhaps related in length to the receptacle in which it will live. In other words, a scoop made to go with a particular bowl, say a sugar scoop with the same capacity as a teaspoon made for a 100 mm (4 in) wide 50 mm (2 in) deep bowl, ought not to have a handle so short that it disappears in the sugar nor so long that it overbalances the bowl.

The fact that the scoop has to hold the loose material while it is being transported is assisted by making the sides of the cup overhang. The amount of overhang does not have to be very much, indeed if it is, it makes it hard to push into the loose material.

Aesthetic considerations are very similar to the goblet particularly with regard to answering curves and the knop. The length of the handle relative to the cup can vary so that, as with a spoon, it can be much longer than the cup because the scoop is not intended to stand on its base.

MAKING A SCOOP

- *Blank*: can be any size depending on function, photos show a sugar scoop made from a blank 41 mm ($1\frac{5}{8}$ in) × 41 mm ($1\frac{5}{8}$ in) × 140 mm ($5\frac{1}{2}$ in).
- *Timber*: practically any close-grained hardwood, as for pestle.
- *Tools*: basic tool kit plus cup chuck or bored headstock spindle, 6.25 mm ($\frac{1}{4}$ in) spindle gouge, 18.75 mm ($\frac{3}{4}$ in) half round scraper, hammer or mallet.
- *Lathe speed I use*: 2250 rpm.

Step one – mounting

As with the mortar you have to mount the scoop blank so that you can hollow out one end, but you do not need to use anything as large as the chucks used for the mortar.

Fig. 62
Sizing with spanner and gouge using spanner just to measure

Indeed, it would be most difficult to get at the handle if you did. Most lathes come with their own built-in cup chuck in the form of the bored headstock – usually bored with a morse taper which is ideal for holding blanks as well as fork centres. If your lathe is not so helpful you can make up your own cup chuck as in the section on mortars, but reduce the scale so that it is only 100 mm (4 in) across and

the internal hole has a morse taper number three.

The blank can be sized for the chuck with a spanner used simply as a measuring device, as in **fig. 62**, or, if you want to make a large number of objects in this way, you can sharpen the spanner with a bevel on the outside of one of its wings and use this to cut the taper, as in **fig. 63**. If you do this you will find that it is necessary to turn the taper nearly

to size because the steel of the spanner is not hard enough to do very much cutting. I carefully drive the blank into the chuck with a hammer because it has a smaller head than a mallet, which therefore allows you to hit different parts of the blank end to adjust its concentricity. **Fig. 64** shows the blank being driven into a cup chuck and **fig. 65** shows it being driven into the lathe headstock.

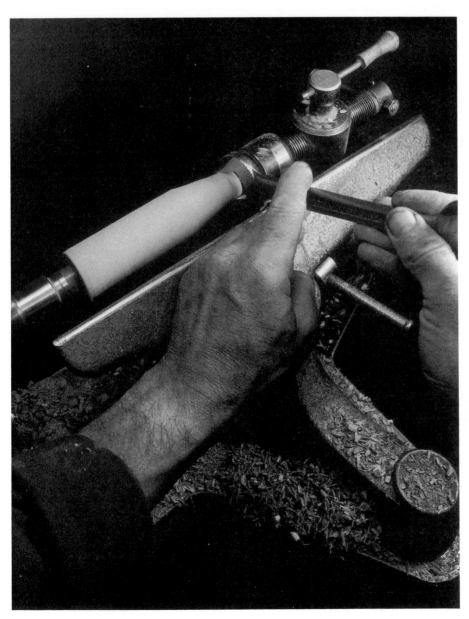

Fig. 63
Sizing with spanner using it as a cutting tool

Fig. 64
Mounting blank in cup chuck with hammer

Step two – roughing out

Use a roughing gouge as for the mortar. You can use a skew for an object this small but I like to use the roughing gouge for the rough work and keep a sharper edge on my skews for that much longer. I use the roughing gouge both to take the blank down to a cylinder and to make the rough shape of the scoop.

Step three – sizing

I make sure all my sugar scoops are of the same size by using a spanner, but because the blank is only supported at one end a sharpened spanner cuts too roughly and it tends to knock the blank out of true. In this instance I therefore use the spanner only as a measuring device.

Step four – shaping

As you can see from **fig. 66**, I shape the outside of only the cup before hollowing it out. If you also do the handle at this stage it will not be strong enough to support the stresses caused by the hollowing process. I use the skew for this in much the same manner as in making the pestle (page 33).

Fig. 65
Mounting blank in headstock with hammer

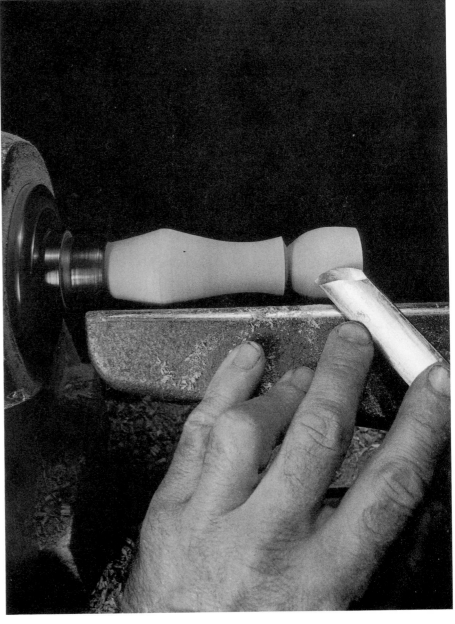

Fig. 66
Shaping cup, not the handle at this stage

Step five – marking the depth

Follow instructions as for marking the mortar on page 38.

Step six – hollowing with gouge

This is done using the same method as with the mortar (page 38), with the left hand supporting the outside of the cup for most of the operation. You should aim to get an even wall thickness because when you remove some of the side to turn it into a scoop it will be quite obvious if you have failed. The walls should be thin enough to thrust into the loose material without being so weak that they will break.

A word of warning: this is a fine line to tread and you will not be able to get a pair of internal callipers into the cup to check your progress. However, if the wood is a light colour such as sycamore or box you will be able to position an adjustable lamp so that it shines on the side of the cup. You can then judge the thickness by the amount of light that passes through. Do be aware, though, that the structure of the wood is such that light passes more easily through the end grain than through any other way. If light shows evenly through all parts of the cup it will be thinner at the end than at the side. I find that because I often use fairly dark woods and because I do not like bending over to see if the light is shining through, I now gauge the thickness by feeling with my finger inside and my thumb outside. If you start feeling at the lip where you can see the thickness and move finger and

Fig. 67
Shaping stem after cup has been hollowed

thumb inside, you can soon feel if they move apart where there is a thick bit.

Step seven – finish with scraper

This is done much as with the mortar (page 40) and is just to get rid of any small ridges that remain after hollowing with the skew. The scraper I use for this work has a larger bevel than normal scrapers and is used pointing upwards so that you get a good clean cut rather than a scrape. The size of the tool is just a few millimetres smaller than the inside of the cup and is carefully

shaped to conform to the required shape. If you sharpen it badly and there are any irregularities in the shape they will manifest themselves as grooves on the inside which can be difficult to sand away.

Step eight – shaping outside

The outside of the bowl can now be shaped precisely, the knop (if any) formed and the stem completed using standard skew techniques as in the pestle (page 33). As you can see from **fig. 67** it may be necessary to support the end of the scoop with one hand while doing the stem, particularly if you want to remove wood at a decent speed.

Step nine – finish

Although your aim should be to get a good finish from the tool, in an item this small you will probably need to do a little sanding with 180 and 220 grit. I cut a standard sheet into eight and fold the eighth into three so that I can get the paper inside the scoop. As with most things I finish scoops with oil and wax.

Step ten – parting off

I part off with the skew as in **fig. 68**. I design most items like these such that they end in a point or a round shape that I can then finish off to the merest point before they break free of the lathe.

Step eleven – shaping the scoop

This can be done in several different ways, though I prefer to use a sanding disc held in a Jacob's chuck, as in **fig. 69**, because when I started making scoops I could not afford a belt sander. Sanding discs are tricky for this purpose because the disc cuts at different rates at different

Fig. 68
Parting off, supporting the scoop with the left hand

Fig. 69
Sanding with a disc in a Jacob's chuck

points on its surface, which can result in a lop sided scoop. I have learnt to press harder on the part to be cut that is nearer the centre, though a belt sander would make life easier. You can do the job with the bandsaw, but on scoops this small the coarse blades I use tend

to shatter the cup. I do use the bandsaw for much larger scoops but I am very careful that the scoops are properly supported. You can also use 80 or 100 grit to remove the bulk of the wood and then progress to a finer paper either on the disc or held by hand.

– 5

BOXES

DESIGN CRITERIA

Turned wooden boxes have an enormous range of uses and offer the turner a chance to exercise his imagination in producing an infinite number of different shapes. Even if the box proves to be quite unsuited for its *prima facie* purpose of containing something, the fact that the lid comes off and reveals a hidden world and the way the grain of the wood is revealed in all its dimensions lend the genre a fascination that has led to it being one of the most collected items of turnery. The fact that a collection can be displayed in a relatively small space is also very attractive to the collector.

Our raw material does place one constraint upon design, which is that if you make a box much over 100 mm (4 in) in diameter the chances are that it will distort in response to a change in relative humidity in the environment at some stage in its life (see next section). This means that, in addition to the fact that seasoned wood of greater size than this is hard to come by, it is better not to design your turned wooden box to contain large objects for the lid will not always fit satisfactorily.

To counter this problem I now rough out all my large boxes, i.e. hollow out the base and lid, but with thicker sides than they will have when finished and leave them for as long as possible before re-turning them.

Even if the wood is well seasoned this gives the tensions in the wood time to relax before it is too late. I always mark the lid and base so that they can be matched up when re-turned.

Fig. 70
Box 50 mm (2 in) × 50 mm (2 in) × 38 mm ($1\frac{1}{2}$ in) in *Robinia pseudoacacia*

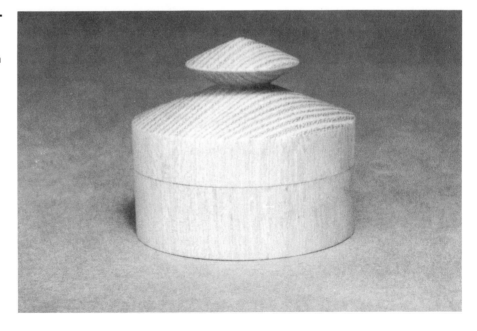

Lid design

There are so many purposes to which boxes can be put that it is not possible for me to cover all the design considerations; in any case working these things out for oneself is half the fun. One thing you will have to decide before you start is whether the lid will fit over the bottom or inside it. For most uses the former is preferable because if a lid has to go inside the bottom it will usually come into contact with the contents (**fig. 71**).

The design of the lid has some other constraints due to the instability of wood. While it is nice to do a box with a lid that is flush with the bottom and that goes over the bottom lip for a good distance (so that it makes a nice pop when it is pulled off!) it is a devil for the user to remove when it has warped slightly! If you can design the lid and box so that the lid is distinct from the bottom and has a groove around the join, or perhaps overhangs the bottom, it will show any distortion less and be easier to

grip when it needs to be taken off. **Figs. 72a–f** show some designs for boxes on this principle. The sources of these designs are transparently Pagoda for **a** and Kremlin for **c**, **d** is derived from the pyramid at Xochicalco in Mexico, **e** is an early British casserole and **f** is a Neolithic pot from Windmill Hill, Wiltshire, England. The last two are in *Interpreting Pottery* by Anne Anderson, and **b** is my design.

The way the lid stays on the bottom by friction is called an interference fit and the exact nature of the contact between the lid and bottom has a profound effect on the ease of use. There is no one way of making the contact that all turners agree is the best, but if the lip on the bottom is parallel and the lid overhangs slightly, the actual point of contact is on a line around the lid rather than a face (**fig. 73**). This should be enough to ensure the lid stays on while not being such a strong fit that it is difficult to remove after probable distortion. In my experience a lid that is a nice close fit as far as I am concerned

may present an impossible trial of strength to someone whose hands are smaller than mine and who has not got the strength of grip I have built up by years of turning. Unfamiliarity with the medium also makes some people afraid to use the strength needed to pull off a tight fitting lid, so I now try to make my lids fit loosely enough for my own hands to open and then ease them some more. This is a matter of fine judgement and experience.

The outside shape of the box ought to be designed before you start because if you make the lid before the bottom as I suggest, you need to know that when it is combined with the bottom the two will make an harmonious whole. You can do a design on paper, if you can draw, or you can do what I do and make a model of the outside shape by turning a solid one in softwood.

This has the double advantage over a drawing of looking exactly like your intended box in three dimensions while also being in wood.

Fig. 71

Two designs of boxes showing effect of lid design on capacity

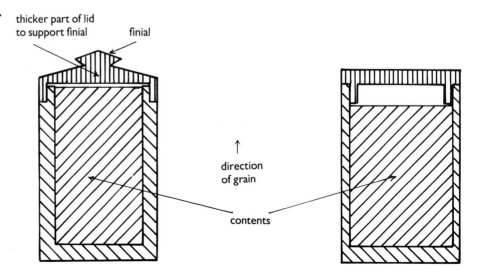

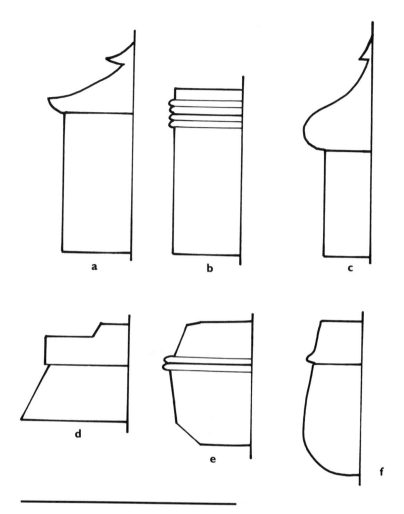

Fig. 72
Box designs with pronounced lips

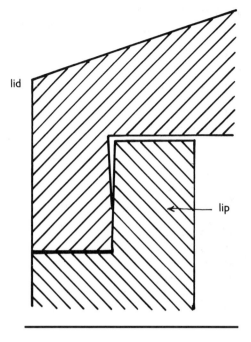

Fig. 73
Box – detail of lid showing fit

Direction of grain

The best way for the grain to be aligned in a box is from top to bottom, because wood distorts less across the end grain than across the side grain. It also distorts more evenly this way and it is less likely to bow. Even so, if the box is more than 100 mm (4 in) across, the distortion possible across the end grain makes it unlikely for the fit to remain satisfactory. It is not a good idea to make a box with the grain running from side to side, because the smallest change in the relative humidity of the atmosphere will cause the wood to shrink or expand more with the grain than across it. There is also the unwelcome possible addition of bowing (**fig. 74** shows the effect of grain direction on box lids).

The added advantage of making a box with the grain running from top to bottom is that it is easier to make the grain on the outside of the box run from the bottom into the lid. This is particularly effective with a strongly-patterned grain such as yew but it is only possible if the wood is straight-grained to start with.

Despite all the above, I sometimes make boxes with the bark on top. In this case the grain runs from side to side so I always select a particularly stable wood such as box as in **fig. 75** and never make them bigger than 50 mm (2 in) across. They have to be made with method two (pages 70 to 72).

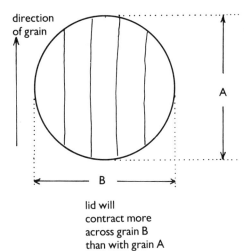

direction
of grain

A

B

lid will
contract more
across grain B
than with grain A

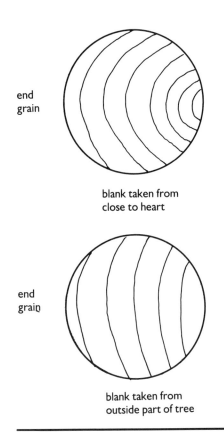

end
grain

blank taken from
close to heart

end
grain

blank taken from
outside part of tree

Fig. 74
Top views of lids showing effects of
different grain directions

Fig. 75
Side grain box in Boxwood with bark on
the top of the lid

MAKING A BOX

□ *Blank*: suggested dimension for
first attempt 50 mm (2 in) ×
50 mm (2 in) × 125 mm (5 in).
□ *Timber*: any straight-grained,
close-grained hardwood. Chose
an easy going timber like
sycamore or maple to start with
but in general avoid any timber
that has an unruly grain or
distorts a lot with changes of
humidity, such as elm. If you can
take your blank from a plank cut
from near the outside of the tree,
so that the grain is running across
the end in straight lines rather
than segments of an arc, this will
also be less prone to warping
(**fig. 74**).

□ *Tools*: basic tool kit plus four-jaw
chuck, collet chuck or cup chuck,
6.25 mm ($\frac{1}{4}$ in) spindle gouge,
12.5 mm ($\frac{1}{2}$ in) straight ended
scraper, hammer or mallet and
internal callipers.
□ *Lathe speed I use*: 2250 rpm.

Mounting

Mount the blank as for mortar (page
35). For method one (**fig. 76**) only
one chuck is necessary, but for
method two, you can either use two
separate chucks or use the body of
the box as a cup chuck for the lid by
making a hole in the end to hold the
finial.

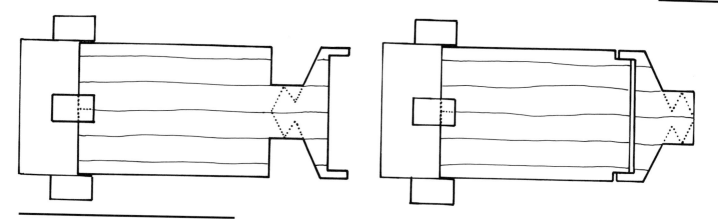

Fig. 76
Box – method one where grain direction in lid is reversed

I will assume that by this stage you will either be sufficiently familiar with the basic techniques not to need reminding about them, or that you are sufficiently familiar with the book to know where to find them.

Once the blank is mounted the sides need roughing out with the roughing gouge.

Method one

This is the quickest and simplest method of making a box, in which the inside of the lid is hollowed out from the end of the blank and then turned around and rechucked on the bottom to turn its top. Because the lid is not in its natural position relative to the bottom the grain will not match up properly unless it is very straight. If you make a knob (finial) for the lid, the lid will be even further removed from its natural position (see **fig. 76**).

1 With the skew (slicing cut) clean up the end of the blank and make it slightly concave so that the outside of the lid will fit flush with the outside of the bottom.

2 With a pencil, mark the depth of the lid on the outside of the blank while it is rotating.

3 With the spindle gouge make a hole in the end the depth of the inside of the lid.

4 Mark the thickness of the sides with a pencil. For a 50 mm (2 in) box, 2 mm ($\frac{1}{8}$ in) is about right, but mark it at least a third wider than this to allow for mistakes in doing the inside and to cater for the smoothing cuts when the lid is fitted.

5 With the same gouge roughly hollow the inside of the lid.

6 Using a square ended 12.5 mm ($\frac{1}{2}$ in) scraper, pointing down and going straight in, do a series of gentle cuts working out from the centre to make the bottom of the lid flat and the sides square. You may find that this leaves a series of ridges on the bottom, but if you use the same tool with its edge parallel to the bottom, starting at the centre and sliding outwards across the bottom, you should be able to get a smooth finish.

7 The sides of the lid should be either absolutely square or slightly overhung. Test this with a pair of internal callipers. While the work is at rest, set them at the internal diameter of the lip of the lid and slide them inwards. If they stick, the sides taper inwards and if they go in, touching the sides, with the same setting as at the lip the sides are square (see **fig. 73**).

8 If the sides of the lid are not the correct angle or are not straight this can be corrected with the skew. Use the point with the side of the tool flat on the rest

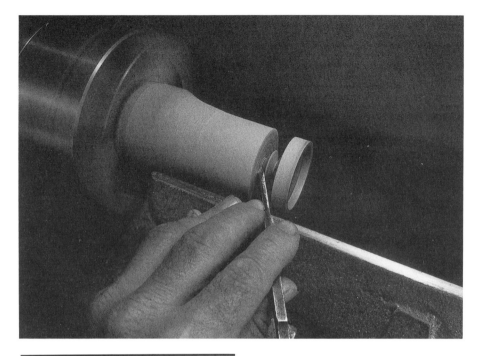

Fig. 77
Parting off lid using skew

Fig. 78
Cutting lip for the lid with skew on its side

and the rest set at centre height as in **fig. 85**, page 72 (method two). Push the tool in horizontally and only take off a little at a time with frequent stops to check with the callipers.

9 If necessary finish the bottom of the inside of the lid with sand paper, but do *not* let it so much as touch the sides because sanding takes off different amounts of wood depending on the grain and will result in the lid becoming not absolutely round.

10 Oil and wax the inside.

11 Check that you have not taken more out of the inside of the lid than intended by using a pencil as a gauge and your thumb as the stop. If the line you drew on the outside is still where the top of the lid will be you can shape the top with a skew according to that line. Should you need to cater for a deeper lid than intended you will have to make the top of the lid on a line nearer the headstock. If you wish to have a finial on the lid you can leave a spigot between the top of the lid and the body, from which to turn it when the lid is reversed onto the end of the blank.

12 Using the skew part off the top (**fig. 77**).

13 As with rechucking the small bowl, measure the inside diameter of the lid with external

callipers, and using a beading and parting tool or the skew on the side, form a very narrow lip for it on the end of the blank (**fig. 78**). Try the lid to see if it fits tightly and when it does, make the lip wider and slightly tapered so the lid tightens up as it goes on.

14 Put the lid on the lip but do not force it or it will either split or be difficult to remove. If it does get jammed, a sharp, thin penknife blade can be inserted in the gap to force it apart. The lid does not have to be flush with the bottom at this stage, indeed it will be easier to remove if it is not; it simply has to be tight enough for you to turn the finial and centred so that the finial is central. Another reason why the fit should be tight at this stage is that the heat generated by turning out the inside may cause the bottom to shrink a little, in which case the fit will become looser.

15 Form the finial with the point of the skew (**fig. 79**). If the lid should start to slip you can put a piece of tissue between the lid and lip. You should also be able to form the finial with one hand on the skew and the other supporting the lid. Sand lightly if necessary and apply your finish.

16 Remove the lid, mark the inside depth and hollow the inside of the bottom part of the box with the spindle gouge.

Fig. 79
Cutting finial with skew point down, slicing cut

17 The shape of the inside depends on the intended use. Where the bottom meets the sides can be either a right angle or curved. If the former, proceed as in the lid with the square-ended scraper. If the latter use a half round scraper.

18 Make the sides straight with the skew on its side.

19 Sand and apply finish to the inside.

20 Refit the lid, and if it is now too loose you can probably extend the lip and taper it so that the lid goes on further. If there is insufficient depth in the lid to allow this you will have to shorten the lip.

21 When the lid is a good fit and the lid and bottom meet perfectly you can shape the outside of the box across the join. If the sides of the lid and base are going to be in a straight line you can run the skew across the join using your utmost care and skill to make the finish from the tool a good one, because if you have to sand the outside much you will find that it will become elliptical and then the lid and bottom will only fit when they are in one position. If the join is not to be flush then this is the time to shape the beads or whatever around the join.

22 Lightly sand outside and apply finish.

69

23 Part off with fluted parting tool, skew or one-sided skew depending on the space available.

24 Finish off the base after fitting the bottom of the box on a spigot as with the lid. (**fig. 80**)

Method two

Only if the grain is dead straight will the grain in the lid match up with the grain in the bottom using the above method. Using method two will make the match better. In this method the lid is made from the wood at the end of the blank so that the knob is on the end (**fig. 81**), and the inside of the lid must be hollowed out after it has been parted from the bottom. The gap between the lid and the bottom has to be as small as possible to make the grain flow through the join.

1 After mounting the blank measure how much wood you need to form the lid and finial and mark this on the end of the blank in pencil.

2 If you have a second three- or four-jaw chuck or a collet chuck, form a spigot on the end of the blank to fit into it. **Fig. 82** shows the spigot being checked for fit in

Fig. 80
Base re-mounted on spigot to finish off bottom

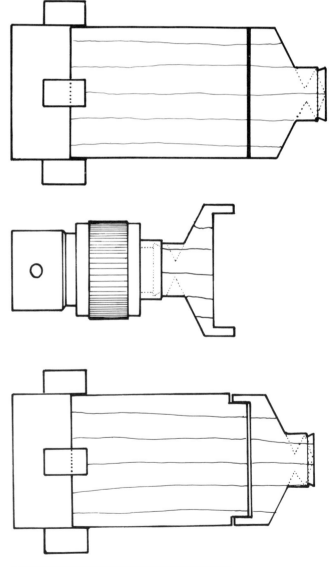

Fig. 81
Box – method two where grain direction in lid goes in same direction as base

the collet chuck. The spigot is a short dovetail formed by a skew. If you only have a cup chuck, it is not a good idea to remove the blank so that you can turn the lid in the same chuck, as it is not always easy to rechuck the bottom centrally. In this case it is better to make a second cup chuck for the lid. The finial will come out of the spigot.

3 Parting off the lid blank can be done with a parting tool but the gap that this makes plus the unavoidable overlap of the lid and lip can be enough to destroy the continuity of the grain. I prefer to use a hack saw with a 450 mm (18 in) coarse blade (**fig. 83**). It is safest to do this at a slow speed as the wood can clog up the teeth and burn if you do not. Should the blade happen to break, the slow speed and the ever present face shield should protect you. I once tried to force matters and caused the blade to break, but because I stopped the lathe immediately the blade did no damage.

4 For the bark-topped box you need to use a four- or three-jaw chuck to mount the lid as in **fig. 84**. Once the lid blank is mounted in the chuck you proceed exactly as in method one. **Fig. 85** shows the skew being used to do the internal sides.

Fig. 82
Trying collet chuck for size on spigot that will be finial of lid

Fig. 83
Parting off lid with hacksaw to reduce gap in grain between lid and base

Fig. 84
Lid mounted on three-jaw chuck for
hollowing

Fig. 85
Cutting inside of lid with skew on side

—6—

RATTLE

DESIGN CRITERIA

When I was doing woodturning at a Craft Centre early in my career, a fellow craftsman suggested that I make a baby's rattle. The only ones I had seen consisted of a hollow shape on a stick containing something loose which rattled, but this seemed too complicated for me to make so I dreamt up the idea of making loose rings around a stem out of one piece of wood (**fig. 86**). They subsequently sold well and my design was accepted onto the Design Index, so that for several years I sold them with that distinctive black and white label which was something of an ego boost to a woodturner in a very small business.

It was not until several years had passed that I discovered that I was not the first to have made such a thing and that there were rattles with loose rings, both in Pinto's collection in Birmingham Museum and illustrated in his book '*Treen and Other Wooden Bygones*'. Since then, wooden rattles have become a common item in many a woodturner's stock-in-trade and it must be said that their design bears more resemblance to mine than the one in Pinto's collection.

It is very hard to make something truly original but it is nice to feel that you have put your own distinctive mark on a traditional genre. It is somewhat ironic that there are many fewer wooden rattles made now because of much more stringent regulations covering the production of children's toys in the European Community. It is just too much trouble for the average woodturner to go through the bureaucratic maze required to get permission to sell such a small item.

Fig. 86
Rattle, 113 mm (4½ in) long, olive ash

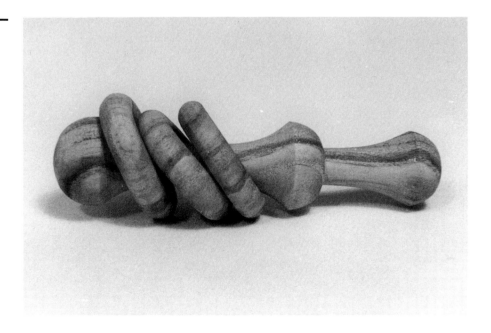

You are allowed to make a rattle other than for sale but you should bear in mind the sorts of design criteria that the officials would look for, and it is best not to make it out of a timber that has toxic properties such as yew. It is also important to make it small enough for the baby not to do itself an injury when it hits itself with it, while making it large enough not to be easily swallowed.

The rattle works best when it has a handle that the baby can hold without interfering with the rattling of the rings. This should be small enough but not too small. The rings should be strong enough not to be easily broken and the timber used should not be easily splintered. There should be no sharp edges. The finish should be non-toxic and easily washable. I have found that no finish at all is the best option.

MAKING A RATTLE

- □ *Blank*: 37 mm (1½ in) × 37 mm (1½ in) × 137 mm (5½ in).
- □ *Timber*: as for pestle.
- □ *Tools*: basic kit plus two one-sided skews or Sorby ring-making tools.
- □ *Lathe speed I use*: 2250 rpm.

Steps one to three

Mounting the blank and roughing out is exactly the same as for the pestle up to step three, pages 27 to 31.

Step four – shaping with skew

Using the skew with a peeling cut reduce the right end of the blank where the handle will be. This should be about one third of the total length but do not make it too thin at this stage because part of it has to be fatter than the internal diameter of the rings, and it is best to leave some room to spare until after you have made them. The first ring is started like any bead: the skew is held with its long face at about 45° to the left of the vertical and with the end of the handle slightly away from the direction of thrust, i.e. about 20° to the axis of the lathe.

The point enters at the top of the bead and you roll the tool over as you form the curved face of the bead (**fig. 87**). When you reach the point where the face is vertical (which would normally be as far as you would go with a bead) you simply carry on so that eventually your tool handle is at right angles to its original orientation and the long

Fig. 87
Cutting right side of ring

face of the tool is at 45° to the right of the vertical, as in **fig. 88**. You cut into the face of the bead to produce an overhang.

You will need to enlarge the vee cut to the right of this overhang to enable the point to get far enough into the under side of the bead, because the tool has two bevels and gets wider as the point goes in. You do this by cutting in with the point of the skew but with the long face of the tool nearly flat on the rest. In other words the right hand bevel is resting on the right face of the vee cut.

The other side of the bead is done in a like manner until you reach a position whereby the undercuts nearly meet. If you can do each side of the bead in one flowing motion you should get a smooth face which needs little sanding, but if you do need to do any, the best moment is just before the two cuts meet underneath so that the ring-to-be is still supported but the final releasing cut is so short that the inside of the ring will need no sanding. **Figs. 89–90** show the finish on both sides of a ring using this method. It is best to avoid forcing the skew into the underhang such that it burns the face of the ring, as it is very difficult to sand away the evidence.

If you leave a large space between the rings the rattle can be made entirely with the skew but it could be rather long. I prefer to make the rings closer together so I came up with the notion of the single bevel skew as already mentioned in project 2, step nine (page 46). This has less bulk following the edge than the normal skew and so does not need such a large vee cut on

Fig. 88
Cutting under right side of ring

Fig. 89
Right side of ring showing finish after separation

Fig. 90
Left side of ring showing finish after separation

Fig. 91
Freeing ring with one-sided skew

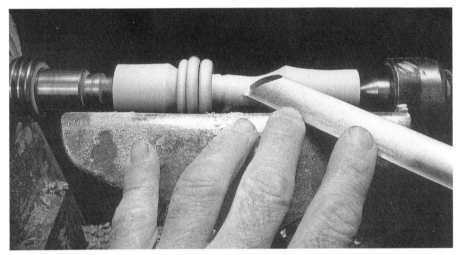

Fig. 92
Smoothing stem, right side using skew
point up, planing cut left hand at rest

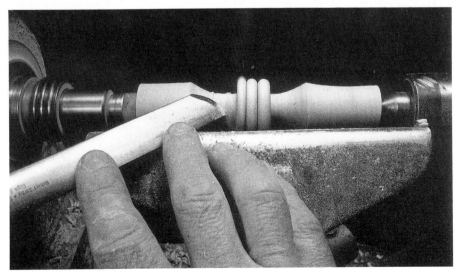

Fig. 93
Smoothing stem, left side using skew point
up, planing cut right hand at rest

either side of the ring. I have made a pair of these, one with the bevel to the right of the point and one to the left so that I can use the former when the point is cutting the right hand side of the ring, as in **fig. 91**, and the latter on the left. The tools are simply converted 12.5 mm ($\frac{1}{2}$ in) skews.

I normally do three rings on a rattle and when they are liberated the stem can be smoothed as in **figs.** 92–93 using the planing cut with the point down. The rings can be held to one side using the hand as in **figs. 94–95** to give you a free run at the stem. **Fig. 96** shows the rattle after sanding.

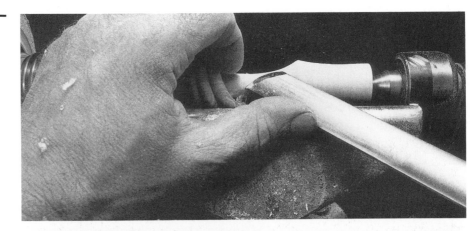

Fig. 94
Smoothing stem, right side, holding rings with left hand at rest to keep stem free

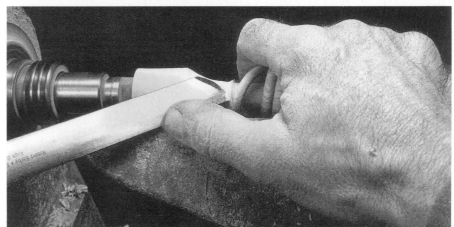

Fig. 95
Smoothing stem, left side, holding rings with right hand at rest to keep stem free

Fig. 96
Rattle on lathe after sanding and before parting off

Making rings with Sorby ring-cutting tools

If you take the trouble to practise and master the skew it is the most satisfying and adaptable tool in spindle turning, but it does take time to get to that degree of expertise. For those who would like to make captive rings without the skew, Robert Sorby Ltd have brought out sets of ring-cutting tools (**fig. 97**). I have tried these out of curiosity and can see that they would enable a comparative novice to make a rattle provided that the clear instructions accompanying each set are followed carefully.

The set comprises a bead forming tool and one left hand and one right hand ring cutting tool. These tools are designed to cut using a scraping action so they must be presented to the work in a line with the centre with the tool held horizontally. I tried to use them with the tool pointing upward to get a more cutting action but this does not work.

To make captive rings with these tools you follow the same sequence as you would using a skew, i.e. you first form a bead and then convert the bead into a ring. You do not have to buy the bead forming tool as you can make the bead with a skew

and then convert it using the ring cutters. The disadvantage of this is that the bead you make might well not be exactly the same size as the ring cutters. In **fig. 98**, I use the bead former as instructed and then the fluted parting tool to make space at both sides of the bead (**fig. 99**). Then the appropriate ring cutter is used to cut the right hand side of the first ring (**figs. 100–102**) followed by the other ring cutter on the other side. I found that it is best to prevent the hollow form from cutting the initial bead by dulling the cutting edge, as suggested in the instructions.

The tools work well enough but

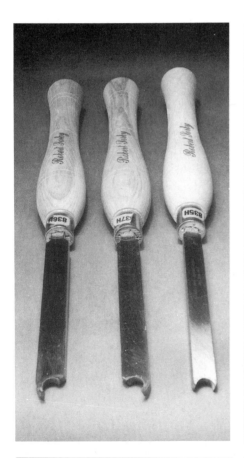

Fig. 97
Set of Sorby 10 mm ($\frac{3}{8}$ in) ring-cutting tools

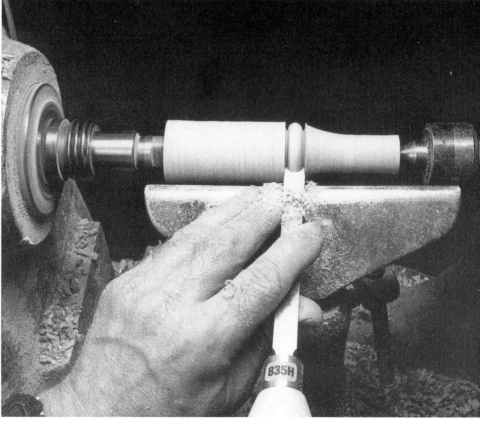

Fig. 98
Forming bead with bead former

Fig. 99
Cutting to side of bead with fluted parting tool

Fig. 100
Cutting right hand side of first ring with one way of holding the tool at the rest

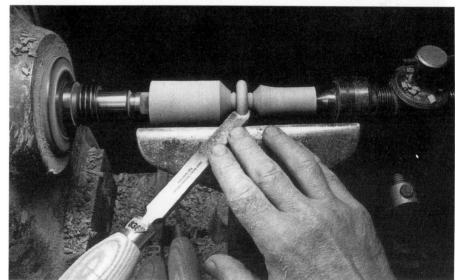

Fig. 101
Cutting right hand side of first ring with an alternative way of holding the tool at the rest

Fig. 102
Cutting right hand side of first ring

do not produce such a fine finish from the tool as a skew so that more sanding is required. It is also more difficult to do the last, freeing cut as finely as with a skew so that you have to sand the inside of the ring after it has been freed. This can be done by wrapping some sandpaper around the stem of the rattle and holding the ring against it while it rotates but this is somewhat time consuming for one who is used to getting a good finish from the tool.

The main disadvantage is that a different set of tools is needed for each size of ring that you wish to make. If you persevere with the skew you will be able to make whatever size of ring you require.

Shaping handle

After you have smoothed the stem of the rattle you can shape the ends and the handle using the skew. Obviously the ends have to be large enough to stop the rings falling off, and I think they should be rounded so that the baby does not damage itself with them. From an aesthetic point of view there should be a similarity of shape between the ends of the stem and the end of the handle. This sort of consistency of design within any given article is one of the hallmarks of good quality.

LACE BOBBIN

DESIGN CRITERIA

There are many different types of lace bobbin, and lacemakers often have their personal preferences. It is therefore sensible to find out exactly what is required before you start to make bobbins. I fear that it is a counsel of perfection to suggest that you learn to make lace before you make bobbins but it would clearly be an excellent idea if you did have the time.

Two of the major types of English lace are Honiton and Bedfordshire. The former requires a plain pointed bobbin because it passes through a loop of thread when connecting part of the motif; it must also be light because very fine thread is used. The latter requires bobbins which act more like weights and can be decorated with beads, coves and even loose rings in addition to having a ring of glass beads on the end. Honiton bobbins are produced commercially very cheaply and are useful for practising fine turning but not very exciting to make. The Bedfordshire types give much more scope for the imagination – they are the only sort I make since I cannot compete with the commercially produced Honiton ones.

There are basic features common to all lace bobbins, as you can see in **fig. 104**. The function is always to hold thread on a stem (known as the neck), passing it around a knob (the head) to the lace being made. The bobbin is gripped in the fingers on the shank. The stem must be slim and smooth but its capacity will depend on the sort of thread being used. If the lace is made from very fine thread, as used in Honiton lace, the capacity must not be too great or the thread will remain on the stem for a long time and get dirty. The head must have a shallow groove in it (known as the short neck) so that the thread can be looped round in a loose knot.

The thistle pattern shown is widely favoured, but do not make any part of the knob sharp as this wears the thread. The body (or shank) of the bobbin has to have a smooth section that can be gripped; it also needs to have a bead on the end large enough for a hole to be drilled through it for the wire on which to thread glass beads.

Fig. 103
Lace bobbin 113 mm ($4\frac{1}{2}$ in) long × 8 mm ($\frac{1}{4}$ in) thick

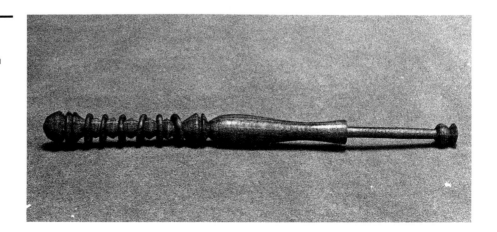

MAKING A LACE BOBBIN

- *Blank*: 9 mm ($\frac{3}{8}$ in) × 9 mm ($\frac{3}{8}$ in) × 125 mm (5 in).
- *Timber*: close, straight-grained and hard such as yew, box laburnum, robinia, ash, oak, hornbeam, spindle, any fruitwood and many ornamental species such as rhododendron that rarely grow large enough for other projects.
- *Tools*: basic kit plus small ring-making tool.
- *Lathe speed I use*: 2250 rpm.

Step one – mounting the blank

Bobbins require a different approach to objects such as a pestle in so far as their delicacy makes the normal forked centre too large to drive them and their elasticity makes them unsuited to the pressure exerted between centres, which would break them. What they require is a chuck that does most of the supporting at the headstock end, such as a Jacob's chuck as shown in the photos or a special lace bobbin cup-type chuck which has a hole specifically designed to take lace bobbin blanks. The Jacob's chuck I use has other uses such as gripping drill bits in the lathe and in theory it is not ideal for lace bobbins since it has three jaws and the blanks have four faces. Despite this it does grip the blanks well enough but if you are worried about gripping four sides in three jaws it only takes a moment to mount the blank in this chuck, turn the other end roughly round and remount the round end.

A revolving centre rather than a dead centre is essential for bobbins because the friction of the latter would quickly burn the end of a bobbin. You can obtain cone centres which are even better, but before you invest in special equipment for bobbins, you have to decide that you are going to make a lot of them.

One thing to remember when mounting a spindle in this way is that the tailstock must be lined up accurately with the centre of the headstock shaft. If it is not, because the spindle being turned is held in place, rather than having the freedom of movement that it would have when mounted on a forked centre, it will fight against the tailstock centre, and when you get to a fine section it will tend to break. If you find out that the centre of the blank at the tailstock end does not accurately align with the other centre, you will probably be able to correct this by putting shims of thin metal in the junction between the bed and the headstock. If this is not possible you may be able to adjust the tailstock. If all else fails contact the manufacturer.

Step two – roughing out

I rough out objects as small as a bobbin with the skew since there is so little material to remove that it does not blunt the tool unduly. I use a modification of the planing cut without much support from the bevel and taking off coarse chips rather than fine shavings.

Step three – sizing

Thickness can be measured with external callipers as with the pestle (page 29), but as you can see in the photos the major features along the length are positioned according to marks on the rest. Most lathes do

Fig. 104
Lace bobbin naming of parts

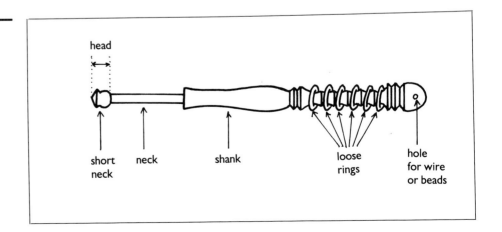

head

short neck

neck

shank

loose rings

hole for wire or beads

not have a rest as short as a bobbin so you either buy a specially-made rest or do as I have done and make your own. I was fortunate to have an old rest which was just a flat piece of iron soldered at right angles to a shaft that fitted my rest support. All I had to do was drill it so that I could attach a piece of hornbeam the shape you see in the photos. Any very hard wood would be suitable but hornbeam is the best I know of for the purpose.

Step four – shaping

The bulk of the shaping is done with the 18.75 mm ($\frac{3}{4}$ in) skew but I like to make my bobbins distinctive by adding six rings. There is no great difference between adding these rings to a lace bobbin and making a rattle except that they are so much smaller. On this scale even a one-sided skew will not get right under the rings so I have made a modified skew as you can see in **fig. 105**. I ground this shape from a piece of square-sectioned tool steel and it took a little experimentation until it worked perfectly for me. You can see it in action in **figs. 106 – 107** and it really works in much the same way as a skew with the point down.

After the ornamental shank has been completed, the long neck must be turned with the skew and you will need to support the work with the hand at the rest as the neck needs to be quite thin and is prone to flexing – it may even break if you do not. There is nothing worse than ruining a lace bobbin at this stage after you have spent all that time and effort making the rings! Now all you need to do is form the head.

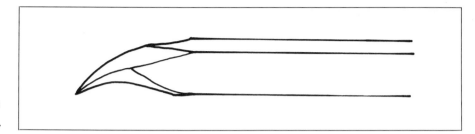

Fig. 105
Modified skew for ring cutting

Fig. 106
Cutting ring left side with modified ring making skew

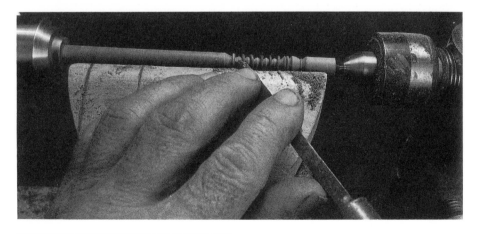

Fig. 107
Cutting right side with modified ring making skew

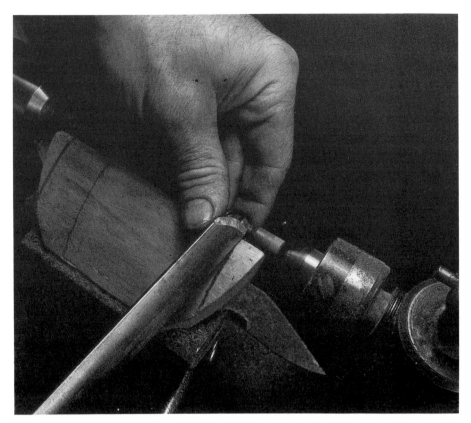

Fig. 108
Parting off, tailstock end leaving small spigot to support bobbin

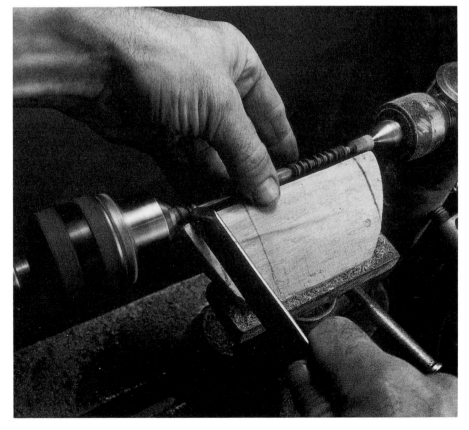

Fig. 109
Parting off, headstock end leaving small spigot to support bobbin

Step five – finishing

Bobbins are so fine and have to be done with such care from such hard wood that they should need little sanding. Indeed, any more than a light touch with a bit of 180 and 220 grit would probably remove the fine details. I use thin strips of cloth-backed abrasives but never wire wool since on the one occasion when I did, it wrapped itself round the bobbin which promptly broke in two. Oil and wax are adequate for bobbins but some lacemakers like a more glossy finish. In general I do not like glossy finishes because the light reflecting off the surface tends to obscure the beauty of the grain, but this does not matter so much in the case of bobbins because they rarely show enough grain for it to matter. To get a glossy finish I use a shellac-based finish specifically made for turning called Crafteeze.

Step six – parting off

Parting off is best done with the skew so that both ends are finished as much as possible on the lathe. This requires the very lightest of touches and the support of the hand at the rest. As you can see from **fig. 108**, start by reducing the tailstock end until there is just enough left to support the bobbin; then reduce the headstock end to a similar diameter (**fig. 109**). Go back to the tailstock end where, if you are careful, it is possible to support the bobbin lightly enough to enable you to part off completely and finish the end with the skew (**fig. 110**), before parting off completely at the headstock end (**fig. 111**).

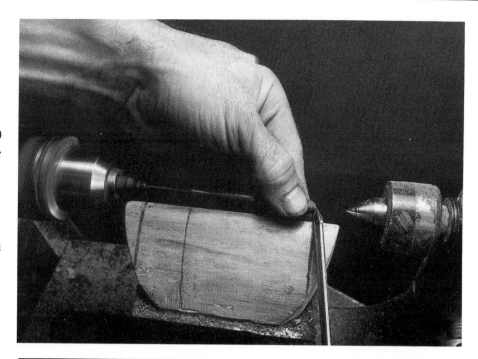

Fig. 110
Cleaning end after freeing it but while it is still rotating by holding it in left hand

Fig. 111
Final parting off at headstock end

Step seven – drilling the end

For a bobbin such as this, the end needs a hole drilled in it through which the wire can pass for the glass beads. I do this by putting a drill bit of the appropriate size in the Jacob's chuck and holding the end of the bobbin against it while steadying my hand on the tool rest. You must not press very hard or the wood will break out at the end of the hole. It is also a good idea to hold the bobbin in such a way that your thumb is not in line with the end of the hole or some impromptu red staining may take place.

Cow and calf

The most elaborate bobbins are those containing baby bobbins such as that in **fig. 112**, which is the same size as an ordinary bobbin. I make these by mounting a bobbin blank in the usual way and then cutting off a short piece to form the end that you can see in **fig. 113**. This is effectively the end of a box and I hollow it out in a three-jaw chuck leaving the mark of the tailstock in the end. The body of the bobbin is hollowed out with a drill bit, slowly, to avoid overheating and cracking the wood and then a lip is formed

on the end to take the lid. The lid can then be fitted and the tailstock brought up to enable the shaping of the rest of the bobbin to take place.

The baby bobbin is turned out of bone from a cow's leg which has been cut into convenient lengths on the bandsaw to release the marrow. It is best to make sure the cow is dead before attempting this. The bone is boiled for hours with frequent changes of water (the first change makes excellent stock) to remove most of the fat which would otherwise go rancid. Bone can be turned with normal turning tools, but it blunts them rather quickly and you need not bother about rubbing the bevel.

Windows can be cut in the body of the big bobbin using a combination of drills, rifflers, carving tools and abrasives.

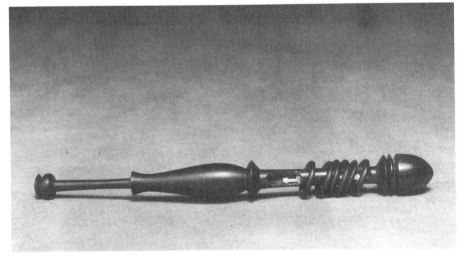

Fig. 112
Cow and calf, same size as ordinary bobbin with bone calf inside

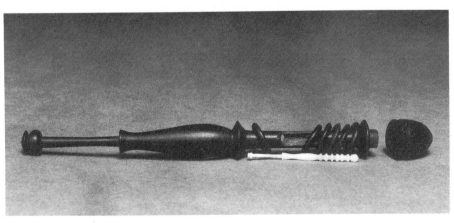

Fig. 113
Cow and calf open showing lid detached

–8–

TRUNNION BOX

DESIGN CRITERIA

Once you have mastered boxes and rattles you have the necessary skills to make a trunnion box (**fig. 115** shows cross-section). I became fascinated by the idea of doing rings within rings after I had been doing rattles and bobbins for several years and this is the entirely functionless result. It is a vehicle for doing as much elaboration as you can and has a great deal of potential for further development. The name trunnion is an engineering term denoting a pin on which anything is supported and was particularly used for the pins which pivoted a cannon on its carriage, so my use of the term is vaguely correct but chosen as much for its sound as its technical accuracy.

Fig. 114
Trunnion box 81 mm ($3\frac{1}{4}$ in) tall × 38 mm ($1\frac{1}{2}$ in) wide in yew

MAKING A TRUNNION BOX

- *Blank*: as illustrated 37 mm ($1\frac{1}{2}$ in) × 37 mm ($1\frac{1}{2}$ in) × 137 mm ($5\frac{1}{2}$ in); it does not matter what size you do, but they tend to be less charming when much bigger than this.
- *Timber*: as for other boxes.
- *Tools*: basic kit plus special tools as in **fig. 116** (the spindle gouge and square-ended scraper are not used in this project).
- *Lathe speed I use*: 2250 rpm, slowing down for the tricky bits.

Step one – mounting the blank

The blank is prepared and mounted like the scoop blank (page 58).

Step two – shaping the top

The first feature to make is the ring on the top of the box using the same techniques used in making the rings on a bobbin (page 83); then shape the top of the box with the skew. The top moves freely around a stem so first you need to make a cut into the top of the box, just below the flange that stops the top ring sliding downwards (**fig. 117**). For this cut

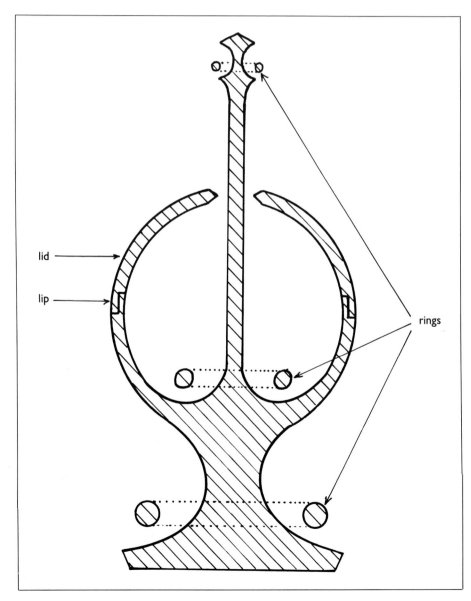

lid

lip

rings

Fig. 115
Trunnion box cross section

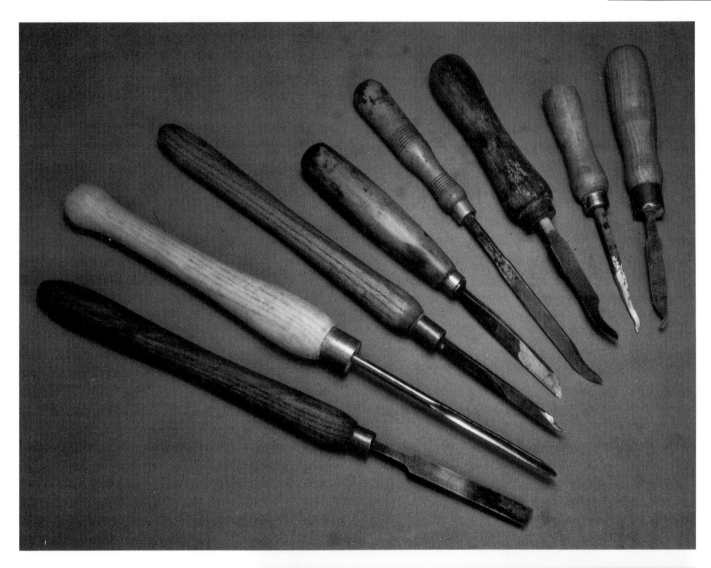

Fig. 116
Set of special tools: (*from bottom*) square
ended scraper, spindle gouge, modified
(ring cutting) skew, two one sided skews,
two round nosed cranked scrapers, square
nosed cranked scraper

Fig. 117
Cutting into top of lid with modified ring
making skew

Fig. 118
Vee cut at base of top where edge of lid will be, using skew

Fig. 119
Hollowing lid with modified skew

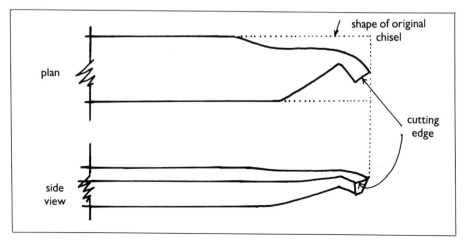

Fig. 120
Square ended cranked scraper ground from straight chisel

use the ring-making skew (page 83) with the point down. You are making the top section of the stem but you do not need to go all the way through the thickness of the lid because you will be cutting from the inside to meet this cut later.

Step three – hollowing the lid

Using the skew, cut into the side at the point where the bottom edge of the lid will be, making a vee (**fig. 118**) and then enlarging it. Bear in mind that the lid must fit over the bottom and therefore the cut at the lower edge of the lid should be at right angles to the axis or slightly overhung. The left face of the vee needs to be cut at about 45° to the axis so that the tools that will hollow the lid can get in through the gap.

I start the hollowing with the adapted skew used for the rings on lace bobbins (**fig. 119**) and then form the lip so that the lid fits over the base. This lip has to be parallel to the axis so you need a tool with a right-angle bend and a square end, which can be ground from an old chisel (see **figs. 116** and **120**). It is necessary to cut the lip (**fig. 121**) before you have taken much out of the inside of the lid so that the cut is well supported. If you were to leave it until the stem had been thinned down you would probably break it.

The lid is now hollowed with a cranked, round-nosed scraper (see **figs. 116** and **122**). As you see, you will need two of these tools, mirror opposites, one for the lid and one for the base. Both have a slight point used to cut into the lid along the

Fig. 121
Cutting lip with cranked, square ended scraper

Fig. 122
Pair of cranked round nosed scrapers

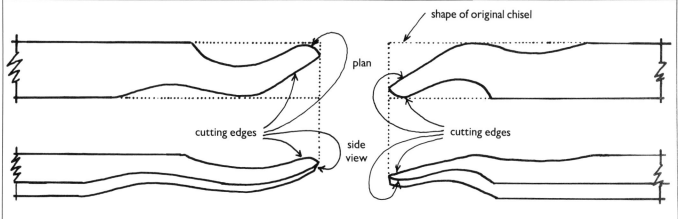

shape of original chisel

plan

cutting edges

side view

cutting edges

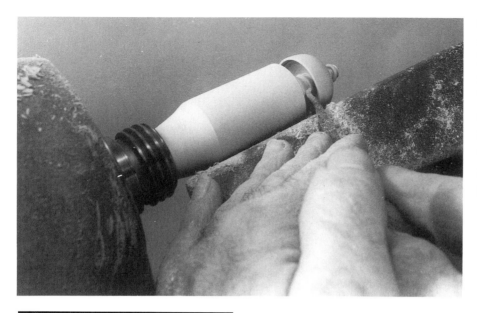

Fig. 123
Cutting stem with cranked, round nosed
scraper

Fig. 124
Ring inside after it was cut with modified
skew

stem and through to meet the cut
started from the outside. You only
have room in the lid to scrape with
this tool so the tip must point down.
The cutting edge is bound to
overhang the rest so you cannot
take a very heavy cut without
causing chatter but because there is
not much timber to remove it pays
to go steady.

As you hollow the inside there is
a tendency for the side of the
scraper to rub the lip, so keep half
an eye on this as you progress to
avoid removing it accidentally. It is
very difficult to judge the thickness
of the lid because it is so small that
you cannot get a pair of callipers
inside. You simply have to go
carefully and judge by eye.

Turn the sides down to the correct
thickness and aim for a good finish
from the tool as you progress
inwards; first, because the sides
will only be supported by a thin
stem, which is not strong enough to
support a final finishing cut when
you have done all the hollowing,
and second, because there is
insufficient room inside for
sandpaper. At least if you cannot get
sandpaper inside no one will be able
to get their fingers in to check the
quality of your finish!

Step four – forming the stem

The stem must be turned with the
inside cutting edge of the scraper as
you hollow (**fig. 123**) so that
eventually you meet the cut in the
top of the lid. It does not need to be

finished at this stage because when the lid is liberated you can hold it out of the way with the hand at the rest to give yourself better access. The tool used on the stem is the ring-forming skew but remember to cater for the internal ring (**fig. 124**). This ring is formed using the same tool in the usual way. Continue the stem into the base so that the ring can sit inside, allowing a lip to be turned on the base to accept the lip on the lid.

Step five – forming the bottom

When you make the lip on the base you should be careful to make it so that the lid fits tightly, because when you hollow the bottom the heat generated will cause it to shrink slightly which will ease the fit. With the lid in position the bottom can be partly shaped to match the top but bear in mind that you must leave sufficient wood to make as many rings as you want to on the bottom stem.

Step six – hollowing the bottom

The bottom is hollowed using the appropriate cranked, round nosed scraper (**fig. 125**) and if your rest is fine enough you may be able to make the job easier by moving the rest in between the lid and base as in **fig. 126**. Once the base is hollowed you can make the base as elaborate as you like (**fig. 127**).

Fig. 125
Hollowing base with cranked, round nosed scraper

Fig. 126
Hollowing base, rest between lid and base

93

Fig. 127
Finished box on lathe

LONG SPINDLES

Long spindles may be chair legs, table legs or balusters. They are the sort of thing that most production turners make and although they rarely feature as exciting examples of the turner's craft they are just as difficult to make as a bowl and more difficult to make at a speed fast enough to be economically viable, largely because the price that people expect to pay for them is so strongly influenced by the cheapness of those produced on a copy lathe. I only make them for high-quality furniture manufacturers whose work warrants a premium price and who do not require the long production runs that justify setting up a copy lathe.

DESIGN CRITERIA

Most of the long spindles I have done have been to the design of the furniture makers who have commissioned the work, which is only right since spindles never stand as objects in their own right but as part of a piece of furniture or a staircase. If you are working to someone else's design or are copying an existing example (as you might be when restoring an antique or repairing a staircase) there are certain techniques that may be used to ensure that your copy is as close to the original as possible, and I deal with these in the next section.

If, however, you want to design your own spindles as part of a piece of furniture or a staircase, there are functional criteria of a basic nature to pay heed to, such as size and length and types of joint. These will depend entirely upon the overall design and are beyond the scope of this book. Suffice it to say that if you convert any given length of square-section stock to a cylinder you do not materially alter its strength. When making a staircase you also need to comply with any statutory requirements such as Building Regulations in the United Kingdom.

With regard to the details of the shapes you give the spindle, this will depend ultimately on what you find agreeable, which will in turn stem from the examples of spindles you have been subjected to, whether you are persuaded to emulate them or react against them! My own taste is for the long subtle curve rather than a great deal of ornamentation, and it must be said that although a lot of elaborate details may be time consuming to turn you can take just as long getting a long curve exactly right. You can also more accurately reproduce the elaborate details than the curve since there are more definite points of reference to measure. Once, however, you do develop your own characteristic style of curve by practising it at the lathe you will find that it will be bound up with your tool technique and will flow from your tools quite readily.

With regard to getting design ideas the study of examples on old furniture and stairs will reap considerable rewards in developing your own taste, but a second-best course of action is to study the examples in *Mouldings and Turned Woodwork of the 16th, 17th and 18th Centuries* (see book list at back). There are certain general principles that I have developed from a study of these and other examples that I think would act as a fairly uncontroversial basis for spindle design.

The vocabulary of design can be as recondite as any other discipline but there are two terms I think could do with being defined before I start. First, a simple curve is an arc of a single circle, ellipse, parabola etc, and second, a compound curve is the amalgamation of the arcs of more than one such circle etc. For example, the profile of a sphere is a simple curve whereas the profile of an egg is a compound curve, composed of the arcs of at least four circles etc.

Simple curves look good as part of a design but are surprisingly rare, while compound curves are more common but are most successful when they are a combination of only a few circles or parabolas etc. Satisfying compound curves flow in a way that seems to have their own logic. There may be a mathematical basis for this but I do not know it and would like to believe that it is more a matter of eye than formula. It is easier to analyse these matters after the shape has been turned than to use them as rules to design a shape but it does seem to me that the human eye (whether as a result of conditioning or as an innate response) finds simple shapes easier on the eye than complex ones and, more explicitly, that where shapes are composed of circles there is a tendency for the eye subconsciously to follow the arc of the circles beyond their manifest extent so that if many different circles are involved the eye gets bored or confused.

The most satisfying way to change from a concave curve to a convex curve is with a definite change of direction such as a shoulder or the punctuation mark of a square or angular bead. The eye is given a signpost that the profile is changing. It is also a good principle to make the shape of the concave curve echo the shape of the convex curve.

All these ideas concern the shape of individual spindles. When fitted to a staircase or a piece of furniture they have to work together with other shapes in a complex way and you have to take into account how you are dividing up the space. I wonder how much thought is commonly given to the way the shapes of balusters affect the space between them and how this varies according to whether they are lined up on the flat as on a landing or when they are lined up on a slope as on the side of the staircase?

As to whether your design includes square sections depends on the joint to be made at the end and your taste but, if it does, it is vital to do the planing square before you turn. It may seem obvious but it was not obvious to me when I did my first set of balusters for my own stairs. I did not have a planer so I decided that I would have less planing to do if I did the turning first and the planing after. What happened was that it was very difficult to plane the square sections to the same centre as the round section and I see the resultant lack of symmetry every day! If you do include square sections in a spindle and you are fitting in with old furniture or stairs, you may like to know that up to and including Victorian times shoulders were not rounded, as is the fashion at the moment and as you can see in the photos.

MAKING A LONG SPINDLE

The example described below is a baluster but it includes many of the features of any long spindle.

☐ *Blank*: 40 mm (1½ in) × 40 mm (1½ in) × 1000 mm (40 in).
☐ *Timber*: any close-grained hardwood or strong softwood such as yew, but avoid curly grain, knots and burrs as they make it hard to turn and less strong. The photos show oak, which is one of the more difficult woods as it is so hard and one of the more awkward woods to get a good finish from the tool.
☐ *Lathe speed I use*: 1330 rpm.

Step one – mounting

Spindles are usually mounted between centres and the problem of flexing, when the wood goes away from the tool, is also common. The usual solution is a centre steady which supports the centre of the work. You can buy these from lathe accessory suppliers or make them yourself as I did out of a couple of ball races and some wood; though in fact I solved the problem by removing the root cause, which was that when turning between conventional centres the wood is held in place by the pressure exerted by the centres, and it is this pressure that causes the wood to flex. If, however, you support the wood at the headstock end with a four-jaw chuck (**fig. 128**) and if the tailstock is correctly aligned, there is no pressure between the centres

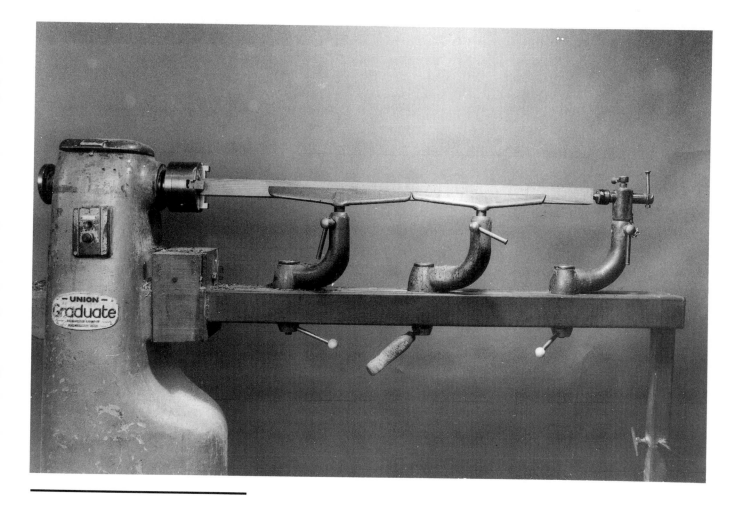

Fig. 128

Spindle blank on lathe held in four jaw chuck

and the only cause of any flexing would be the reaction of the wood to the tool which is easily counteracted by the use of the hand at the rest. This is quicker and more flexible than setting up a steady.

When turning a long spindle there are obvious advantages in having a rest as long as the piece of turning, because you can do the whole length in one sweep of the tool and you do not have to keep stopping the lathe to move the rest. You can buy long tool rests up to 900 mm (35.5 in) long but I have saved myself this expense by using the two rests I have available because I have two lathes of the same make. When lined up carefully there is no gap between them (**fig. 129**) and if I want to get in close to any detail I can remove

one of the rests and adjust the other accordingly.

It is particularly important not to move the rest while the work is rotating when turning work that includes square-sections, because it is so easy to catch the square edges and so hard to restore them once damaged. They are also particularly hard on the fingers.

Step two – marking out

When doing a spindle such as this I mark out the limits of the square sections before mounting the work by measuring the sections and drawing lines across the blank at the relevant points using a pencil and try-square. If you have several identical ones to do it is best to lie them side by side on the bench and

mark them all at the same time by drawing lines across them all. You may find that a line on one face will be visible when the work is rotating, but I make sure that the line is clear by drawing lines on two faces. It also sensible at this stage to look carefully at the wood for any flaws in case they can be included in a section of the blank that will be turned away.

Step three – shaping

Before you can rough out the round sections you must cut the shoulders so that you have clean cuts at either end of the round bits. I use a skew for this (**figs. 130–131**), starting a vee cut and then gradually enlarging it by making a sloping cut at the side that is going to be

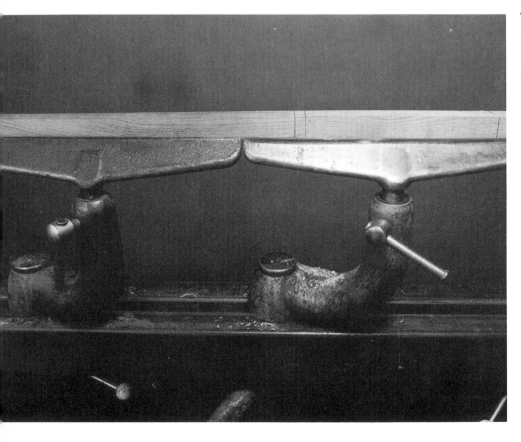

Fig. 129
Blank close up showing no gap between rests

98

Fig. 130
Starting vee cut with 25 mm (1 in) skew
point up

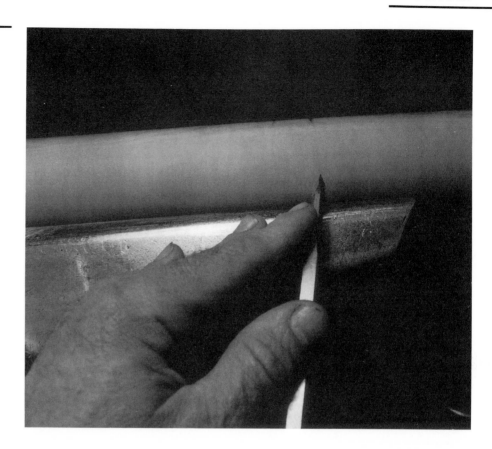

Fig. 131
Cutting to left of vee

rounded and a right-angled cut at the shoulder end. In the case of the extreme ends of the round sections I round off the shoulders as in making a bead (**fig. 132**) except that instead of resting the skew on the top of the bead (which is not possible because the section is still square) you just have to line up the tool as if it were resting on the bead, something that only comes with experience. For the square flange in the middle a right-angled cut is called for which is quite difficult to

achieve so that the sides of the flange are completely flat. It can only be done if the bevel of the skew is precisely lined up with the side of the flange.

When the ends of the sections to be rounded have been established, the parts in between can be roughed out as on any spindle (**fig. 133**).

After the round parts have been roughed out they can be smoothed with a skew using a planing cut as in **fig. 134**. As you can see the tool can be held in place with the heel of the

hand at the rest while the fingers are looped over the work to keep it steady against the cutting edge. When you have a reasonably smooth, straight cylinder between the square sections (known as 'pommels') the beads at each end can be marked using dividers set to the distance between the end of the square section and the far side of the bead. Naturally you must avoid allowing the tip of the dividers to come into contact with the square section.

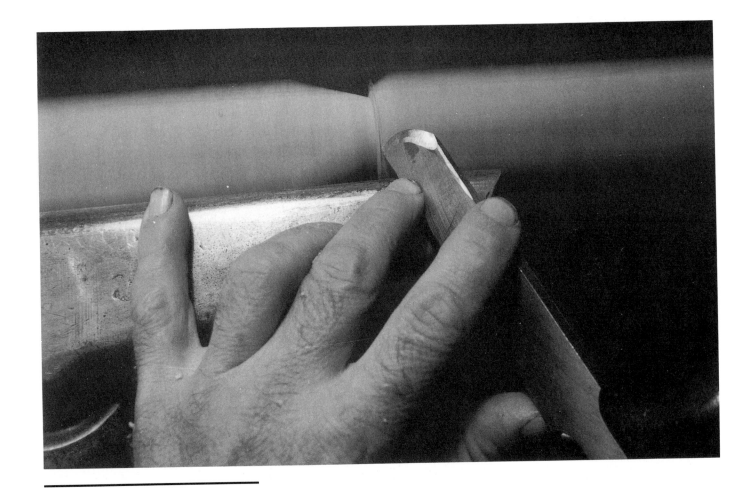

Fig. 132
Rounding shoulder, note how the right hand end has blurred edges because it is square

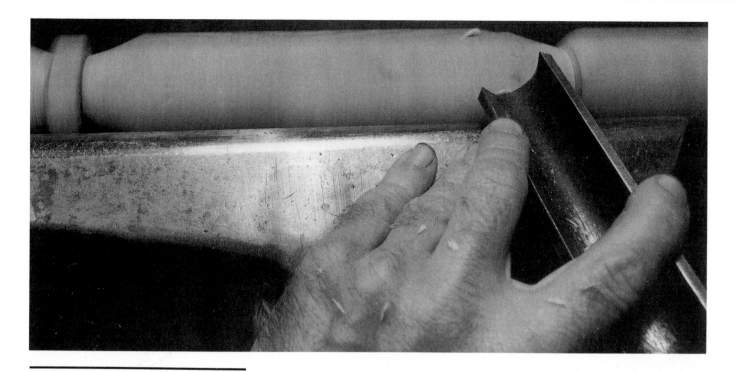

Fig. 133
Roughing out with roughing gouge

Fig. 134
Planing cut steadying tool and spindle with
left hand

The cove between the bead and the square section can be cut initially with the skew by enlarging a vee cut (**fig. 135**), but even though the skew can be used to penetrate quite deeply into the bottom of the cove by raising the handle end and cutting with the edge well below the rest, it is best to round off the bottom of a narrow cove like this using a 6.25 mm ($\frac{1}{4}$ in) spindle gouge as in **fig. 136**. If you want all the coves to be the same depth they should be measured using external callipers, but it is not always necessary to get everything exactly the same on a set of spindles, as slight differences really do add to the charm of hand-turned work. That isn't just an excuse, really it isn't.

Now the curved parts between the beads can be shaped using a skew as in **figs. 137–138**. Using the point down enables quite a heavy cut for the removal of bulk and supporting the work with the hand at the rest helps to keep the cut smooth. Where the design includes square sections, particularly in the middle, as in the photos, great care must be taken to hold the hand as far away from the work as possible to avoid losing skin on the edges of the wood.

I usually judge the shape of the curve by eye with the fattest bits being the maximum thickness of the blank and the thinnest being the same as the bottom of the cove. If you have difficulty with judging this by eye it is an easy matter to cut a template out of hardboard or plywood and hold it against the work at regular intervals to check

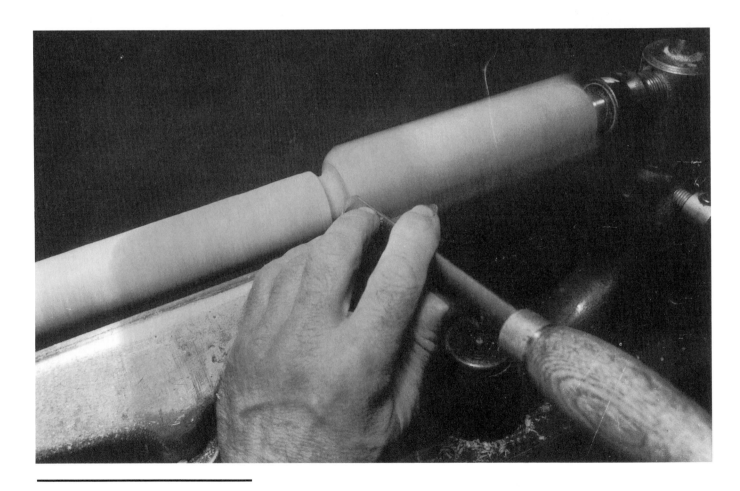

Fig. 135
Hollowing bead with 19 mm ($\frac{3}{4}$ in) skew handle end raised

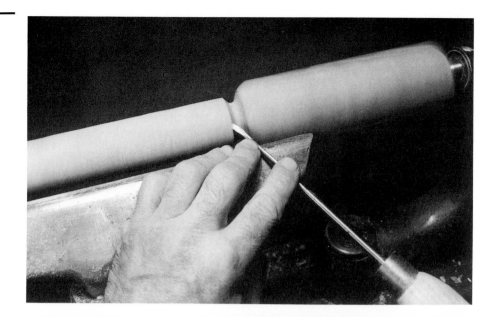

Fig. 136
Hollowing bead with spindle gouge

Fig. 137
Planing cut point down using hand at rest
to steady work and tool but keeping clear
of square section

progress. For smaller pieces or particularly fiddly details where you do not expect to be repeating the shape very often, a commercially made profile gauge composed of a number of sliding steel rods is particularly useful.

It is best to turn the end furthest from the headstock first because the rotational force is transmitted through the part nearest the headstock and this needs to be left as strong as possible for as long as possible.

Very often the point down cut will produce a smooth finish from the tool, but if it does not, it is always worth trying the cut in the opposite direction: the trend of the grain may be more conducive to clean cutting one way more than another but if this does not work it may be that the cut with the point up will work, as in **fig. 138**. You should always check that the tool is perfectly sharp for the final cut but if even this fails to produce a good clean cut try applying a little oil or water to the work (depending on which is compatible with the

eventual finish) before taking a thin cut. Sometimes with particularly curly grain I find that I succeed better with a 6.25 mm ($\frac{1}{4}$ in) bowl turning gouge. Even if the tool leaves a succession of small ridges these are easier to sand away than a rough piece of grain.

In the case of the baluster in the photo I wetted the wood with water and managed to get the finish you can see in **fig. 139**, with the skew cutting heel down going in both directions according to how the wood dictated.

Fig. 138
Planing cut point up to see if this cuts cleaner

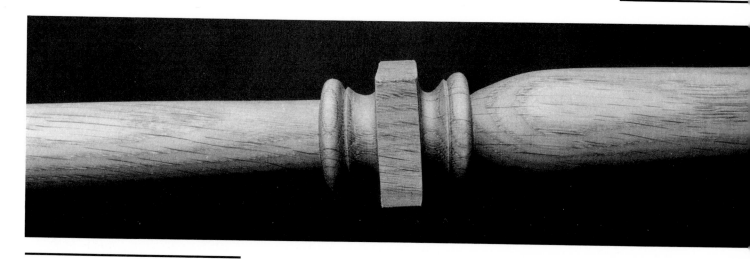

Fig. 139
Close up after skew

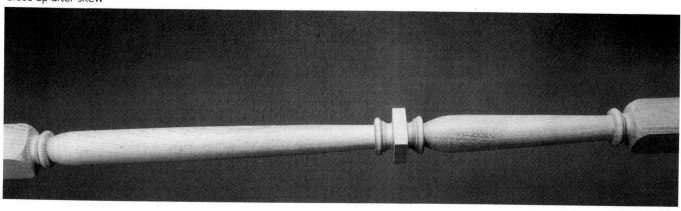

Fig. 140
After 180 grit sanding

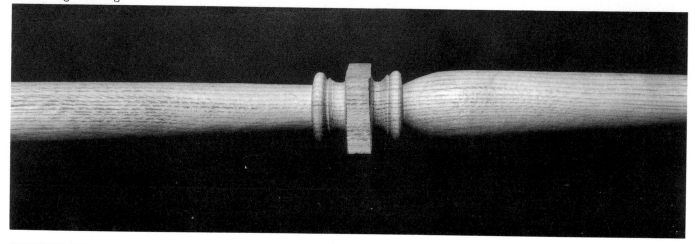

Fig. 141
After 240 grit sanding

Step four – finishing

Sanding spindle work requires the utmost care to avoid losing the crisp outlines achieved with the tool. Fold the paper in three and work up to a bead along a straight section, keeping the paper moving all the time to reduce the grooves that can be left. Hold the paper at right angles to a bead and move downwards from the top using the edge to get into the sharp shoulders and pressing the paper against the work with the fingers and thumb. Start with the finest grade you need and only if this fails go to a coarser grade. In the photo I started with 180 grit, **fig. 140** shows the result, and then progressed to 240 grit (**fig. 141**).

Spindles are usually varnished or painted after they have been assembled because the finish needs to match the piece as a whole. If you have to do a production run for a customer, it pays to find out the standard to which the spindle needs to be finished to avoid spending longer on it than necessary.

AFTERWORD

When examples of spindle turning appear in exhibitions they may well be beautifully finished and put together but they often look old-fashioned. I think this is because we have such a rich heritage of turned chair legs, table legs and balusters, (if not in our own homes, certainly in stately homes and museums) that the turner finds it hard to be original. The fact that the spindle is almost always functional, has both ends performing a role and is made out of severely symmetrical stock certainly restricts design possibilities.

One certain way to break out of the mould is to reduce the amount of ornamentation on spindles and develop your own characteristic curves. If you rely on this and good proportions it should be possible to drag spindle turning out of the Victorian era and straight into the twenty-first century.

There is much more scope for originality in the design of open ended spindles such as the goblet because of the liberating effect of the hollowed end; but boxes, as well as being the greatest technical challenge, also offer the greatest opportunities for innovation and these are being exploited with great vigour and imagination. I have only scratched the surface of box design in this book but I have tried to give sufficient basic techniques and enough of my own design ideas to stimulate the reader into further explorations of this potentially exciting area of the craft.

USEFUL ADDRESSES

EQUIPMENT SUPPLIERS

End Grain Sealer, Crafteeze

Craft Supplies Ltd
The Mill
Miller's Dale
Buxton
Derbyshire SK17 8SN
England

Craft Supplies USA
1287 East 1120 South
Provo
UT 84606

Mobilcer C

Mobil Oil Co Ltd
Mobil House
54/60 Victoria St
London SWIE 6QB
England

Axminster Chuck

Axminster Power Tool Centre
Chard Street
Axminster
Devon EX13 5DZ
England

Lathes

LRE Machinery & Equipment Co
Bramco House
Turton Street
Golborne
Warrington WA3 3AB
England

Craft Supplies and Craft Supplies
USA as above

Axminster Power Tool Centre as
above

Tools

Robert Sorby Ltd
Greenland Rd
Sheffield S9 5EW
England

Henry Taylor (Tools) Ltd
The Forge
Lowther Road
Shefield S6 2DR
England

Jerry Glaser Co., Inc
P.O. Box 2417
Newport Beach
Calif. 92663
USA

Lathe suppliers as above

Airstream dust helmets

Equipment suppliers as above plus

Airstream Dust Helmets
16 Division St W
Elbow Lake
MN 56531
USA

RECOMMENDED READING

Mouldings and Turned Woodwork of the 16th, 17th and 18th Centuries, Tunstall Small and Christopher Woodbridge, Stobart and Son Ltd London, 1987

Pillow Lace and Bobbins, Jeffrey Hopewell, Shire Publications Ltd, 1977

Interpreting Pottery, Anne Anderson, B.T. Batsford Ltd, 1984

The Modular, LeCorbusier, Faber, 1962

Theory of Design, Peter C. Gasson, B.T. Batsford Ltd

A Potter's Book, Bernard Leach, Faber and Faber, 3rd edit. 1976

Turning Wood, Richard Raffan, The Taunton Press, 1985

Turning Projects, Richard Raffan, B.T. Batsford Ltd, 1991

Treen and Other Wooden Bygones, Edward H. Pinto, G. Bell and Sons, 1969

Hand or Simple Turning: Principles and Practice, Holtzapffel's Turning and Mechanical Manipulation Vol 4, John Jacob Holtzapffel, Dover New York (Constable UK), 1991

INDEX